The Apologetics of Jesus

The
Apologetics
of Jesus

A Caring Approach to Dealing with Doubters

Norman L. Geisler
Patrick Zukeran

BakerBooks

a division of Baker Publishing Group
Grand Rapids, Michigan

© 2009 by Norman L. Geisler and Patrick Zukeran

Published by Baker Books
a division of Baker Publishing Group
P.O. Box 6287, Grand Rapids, MI 49516-6287
www.bakerbooks.com

Printed in the United States of America

Library of Congress Cataloging-in-Publication Data

Geisler, Norman L.
    The apologetics of Jesus / Norman L. Geisler, Patrick Zukeran.
       p. cm.
    Includes bibliographical references (p.   ).
    ISBN 978-0-8010-7186-7 (pbk.)
    1. Jesus Christ—Teaching methods. 2. Apologetics. I. Zukeran, Patrick. II. Title.
BT590.T5G37 2009
232.9′04—dc22
                                            2008032604

To all my apologetics students for fifty years from whom I have learned so much, with the greatest appreciation.

Norman Geisler

To my partners in ministry who support, pray, and serve alongside me in the defense of the gospel of Christ. I repeat the words of Paul in Philippians 1:3–5: "I thank my God every time I remember you. In all my prayers for all of you, I always pray with joy because of your partnership in the gospel from the first day until now."

Patrick Zukeran

Contents

Acknowledgments

To my dear wife, Barbara, who for over half a century has been my loyal companion and meticulous proofreader, I express my deepest gratitude. In addition, I give thanks to my faithful assistants Bill Roach and Joel Paulus, for their crucial help in preparing this manuscript.

Norman Geisler

Introduction

That Jesus is one of the greatest teachers who ever lived is not in dispute, even by most non-Christians who are aware of his teachings. Certainly he is the ultimate model for Christian teaching. Given this fact, we can only conclude that Jesus was also the greatest apologist for Christianity who ever lived.

Apologetics comes from the Greek word *apologia*, which means a defense. The apologist uses reason and evidence to present a rational defense for the Christian faith. Jesus was continually confronted with the need to defend his claims to be the Messiah, the Son of God. So by definition, he was an apologist.

Despite the fact that Jesus was an apologist and that by common consent he was probably the greatest teacher ever, it is strange indeed that no one has written a major work on the apologetic methods of Jesus. This book is an attempt to correct that serious omission.

Those who oppose apologetics in favor of a leap of faith without evidence will be disappointed in Jesus. Nowhere does he call on anyone to make an unthoughtful and unreasoned decision about his or her eternal destiny. Everywhere Jesus demonstrates a willingness to provide evidence for what he taught to every sincere seeker. Indeed, the Law and the Prophets, which Jesus came to fulfill (Matt. 5:17), inform us of a God who says, "Come now, let us reason together" (Isa. 1:18), and exhorts us to test false prophets (Deut. 13:1–5; 18:14–22). And those who were taught by Jesus exhort us to "give the reason for our faith" (1 Peter 3:15) and not to make a *leap of faith in the dark* but rather to take a *step of faith in the light*—in the light of the evidence he has provided in nature (Rom. 1:19–20), in our hearts (Rom. 2:12–15), and in history (Acts 17:30–31).

Jesus's apostles used apologetics in their preaching from the beginning of their ministry. For instance, Paul tells the Philippians, "I am appointed for the defense of the gospel" (Phil. 1:16 NASB). The apostle Jude (Jesus's half brother) exhorts us to "contend for the faith that was once for all delivered to the saints" (Jude 1:3 NRSV). The classic text of 1 Peter commands us, "Sanctify the Lord God in your hearts, and always be ready to give a defense [*apologia*] to everyone who asks you a reason for the hope that is in you" (1 Peter 3:15 NRSV), and Acts 1:3 (NKJV) speaks of Jesus presenting himself with "many infallible proofs."

Based on the empty tomb and the resurrection, Peter argues that Jesus is the long-promised Messiah (Acts 2:29–36). In Acts 3 the healing of a man lame from birth is provided in the name of Jesus and as evidence he is the resurrected Messiah. The apostles use apologetics with the heathen at Lystra in Acts 14, arguing from nature that God "did not leave himself without witness" (v. 17 RSV). In Acts 17 Paul uses apologetics when speaking to Jews who had not accepted Jesus as their Messiah. He "reasoned with them from the Scriptures [the Old Testament, God's special revelation], explaining and demonstrating that the Christ had to suffer and rise again from the dead" (vv. 2–3 NKJV). Later in the same chapter he reasons with the Greek philosophers on Mars' hill, beginning with God's general revelation and arguing for the existence of God from the things he had made (vv. 22–28).

Giving evidence for God and Christ is a common activity of the Old Testament prophets. Moses is provided with miraculous evidence of his claim to be God's spokesperson (Exod. 4:1–13), as is Elijah (1 Kings 18) and other prophets. God also gives evidential tests for a prophet in Deuteronomy 13 and 18. Apologists have long appealed to these events as a basis for their endeavors. In view of this, it is amazing that there is no major work available on the master apologist himself, the Lord Jesus Christ.

Anyone who makes a truth claim—to say nothing about a claim to ultimate truth (John 14:6)—must provide evidence for that claim. Jesus does exactly that, and in so doing, he provides a pattern for apologetics that is of great value to the contemporary defender of the Christian faith. What could be more helpful than the model of the Master?

First, we will look at Jesus's use of testimony as an apologetic (chap. 1), followed by his use of miracles (chap. 2) and the resurrection (chap. 3) to support his claims. Being the Logos (reason) of God, it is understandable that Jesus utilized human reason in his teaching (chap. 4). But hidden in his parables is a powerful apologetic for his deity (chap. 5). Of course, he also employs apologetics in his discourses (chap. 6). His appeal to prophecy is also offered as a strong indication of his supernatural claims (chap. 7). Implied in his teachings are indications of how Jesus would have approached the subject of arguments for God's existence (chap. 8). Of course, an answer must be given for those who take some of Jesus's statements out of context in an anti-apologetic way (chap. 9). And one cannot neglect the fact that Jesus not only had an apologetic but that his life was also an apologetic (chap. 10). In this connection, it is important to show the role of the Holy Spirit in convincing people of the truth of Christ (chap. 11). Finally, from all of the above we attempt to construct an apologetic method (chap. 12). I hope this will cast light on which of the current apologetic systems is closest to that of Jesus's approach.

The study of Jesus's apologetics yields some rewarding results. It provides an example to follow, since he is the greatest of apologists. In so doing, such a study benefits not only the apologists but also every Christian who wants to be an effective witness for Christ to an unbelieving world.

1

Jesus's
Apologetic Use of
Testimony

A man lay ill for thirty-eight years beside the pool of Bethesda, along with a multitude of sick and lame individuals. Suddenly a stranger walks up to this man and asks him a strange question: "Do you want to get well?" As the lame man begins to explain his situation, the stranger orders the man: "Get up! Pick up your mat and walk!" (John 5:8). Immediately strength enters his legs and he rises and walks, carrying his mat as the stranger ordered. Soon afterward the Pharisees arrive, and a conflict ensues.

What should have been a moment of rejoicing turns into a serious interrogation. The Jewish leaders confront Jesus seeking a reason and opportunity to kill him. Instead of praising God for the healing of the lame man, the focus of the Jewish leaders is on the fact that Jesus has violated their Jewish tradition.

In his defense, Jesus presents some of the clearest and strongest teachings regarding his nature as the divine Son of God. Leon

Morris states, "Nowhere in the Gospels do we find our Lord making such a formal, systematic, orderly, regular statement of His own unity with the Father, His divine commission and authority, and the proofs of His Messiahship, as we find in this discourse."[1] It is these very claims of divinity that lead to the hostility and eventual death of Jesus.

Jesus's Apologetic of Witnesses in John 5

Jesus's response can be divided into three sections. The first section, John 5:16–18, records, "So, because Jesus was doing these things on the Sabbath, the Jews persecuted him. Jesus said to them, 'My Father is always at his work to this very day, and I, too, am working.' For this reason the Jews tried all the harder to kill him; not only was he breaking the Sabbath, but he was even calling God his own Father, making himself equal with God."

Jesus claims that he is the divine Son of God and therefore the Lord over the Sabbath. His defense is his intimate and special relationship with the Father. Jesus partakes of the divine nature and acts in complete obedience and unity with God the Father. Jesus states that the Father is always at work in sustaining the universe, and because of his close relationship, he does this work as well. Jesus also calls God "my Father" in a special sense. The Jews understand God to be their Father, but Jesus means something unique in his relationship with God the Father. He is stating that he is of the same divine nature. Upon hearing this, the Jews consider Jesus not only a violator of the law but a blasphemer as well.

In the second part of Jesus's response (John 5:19–24), he declares:

> I tell you the truth, the Son can do nothing by himself; he can do only what he sees his Father doing, because whatever the Father does the Son also does. For the Father loves the Son and shows him all he does. Yes, to your amazement he will show him even greater things than these. For just as the Father raises the dead and gives them life,

even so the Son gives life to whom he is pleased to give it. Moreover, the Father judges no one, but has entrusted all judgment to the Son, that all may honor the Son just as they honor the Father. He who does not honor the Son does not honor the Father, who sent him. I tell you the truth, whoever hears my word and believes him who sent me has eternal life and will not be condemned; he has crossed over from death to life.

Here Jesus affirms that he cannot act independently of the Father. The things that the Father does, the Son does too, not in imitation but in virtue of his sameness of nature.[2] Jesus does not act from his own initiative but in perfect union of will with the Father.

This union is illustrated in the authority to give life. It was understood that the Father raises individuals from the dead. In the same way, Jesus claims authority to give life (v. 21). From the authority to grant life, Jesus states that he is given the authority to judge all things (v. 22). The Jews believed that they would stand before the Father on judgment day, but here Jesus states that the authority to judge has been delegated to the Son.[3] The Jews understood that eternal life rested on their positive response to God's Word; Jesus states that eternal life rests on their response to him and his Word. He has the authority to grant eternal life (vv. 24–27). In claiming authority over these realms, Jesus is proclaiming his equality with God. In fact, the two are so united that failure to honor the Son also means a failure to honor the Father (v. 23).

Such extraordinary claims offend his audience, and Jesus understands their mind-set. According to Old Testament law, a person's own testimony is not valid in a Jewish court of law. A testimony is valid only if there are two or three witnesses who testify to the truth of an individual's claims (Deut. 19:15). Jesus knows that these people need not only solid testimony to confirm his claims but also testimony that will convict them of their error regarding their understanding of him. In this third section, Jesus presents an apologetic defense using the testimony of key witnesses to uphold the claims he has made of himself. He declares:

If I testify about myself, my testimony is not valid. There is another who testifies in my favor, and I know that his testimony about me is valid.

You have sent to John and he has testified to the truth. Not that I accept human testimony; but I mention it that you may be saved. John was a lamp that burned and gave light, and you chose for a time to enjoy his light.

I have testimony weightier than that of John. For the very work that the Father has given me to finish, and which I am doing, testifies that the Father has sent me. And the Father who sent me has himself testified concerning me. You have never heard his voice nor seen his form, nor does his word dwell in you, for you do not believe the one he sent. You diligently study the Scriptures because you think that by them you possess eternal life. These are the Scriptures that testify about me, yet you refuse to come to me to have life.

I do not accept praise from men, but I know you. I know that you do not have the love of God in your hearts. I have come in my Father's name, and you do not accept me; but if someone else comes in his own name, you will accept him. How can you believe if you accept praise from one another, yet make no effort to obtain the praise that comes from the only God?

But do not think I will accuse you before the Father. Your accuser is Moses, on whom your hopes are set. If you believed Moses, you would believe me, for he wrote about me. But since you do not believe what he wrote, how are you going to believe what I say?

John 5:31–47

Jesus's Apologetic Use of Five Witnesses

In his defense, Jesus states that there are five witnesses who testify on his behalf: John the Baptist, his own works, the Father, the Old Testament Scriptures, and Moses (John 5:32–46). Jesus uses the word *testify* (or *testimony*) ten times in this passage. An important aspect of his apologetics involves confirmed testimony or witnesses.

Another key Greek word in this passage is *martyria* (meaning *testimony* or *witness*), which John uses five times. It appears eighteen times in the Gospels: fourteen times in John, three times in Mark (14:55–56, 59), and once in Luke (22:71). The noun *martys* is used five times in the Gospels: twice in Matthew (18:16; 26:65), once in Mark (14:63), and twice in Luke (11:48; 24:48).[4] It refers to a person who gives a witness, declaration, or confirmation of the facts used of eyewitnesses in a legal context.

The English verbs *testify* and *bear witness* are translations of the same Greek verb: *martyreo*. In the Gospels this verb is used thirty-five times: thirty-three instances in the Gospel of John, one in Matthew (23:31), and one in Luke (4:22). It occurs most frequently in John in reference to the witness to the person of Christ as the eternal Son of God (John 1:15; 5:36–47; 8:12–18).[5]

The noun form *martyria* (witness) refers to the testimony given about a person, and it is used fourteen times in the Gospel of John because of that book's significant theme of trial and witness. On several occasions in this Gospel, Jesus is on trial as in a courtroom and presents his witnesses to testify that his claims are true. As mentioned earlier, Old Testament law requires that "by the mouth of two or three witnesses the matter shall be established" (Deut. 19:15 NKJV). John 5 presents one of the most important confrontations, and on this occasion Jesus presents his five witnesses: John the Baptist (vv. 33, 35), his own works (v. 36), God the Father (vv. 36–38), the Old Testament Scriptures (v. 39), and Moses (vv. 45–46). In a court case, the strength of the defendant's case is determined by the integrity and credibility of the witnesses who are called forth. Jesus presents these five witnesses of impeccable character; he could not have called upon any stronger testimony.

The Witness of John the Baptist

The Jews are well aware of John the Baptist, as shown in John 1:19–28, which records them sending a delegation to question him as to his identity. Matthew 21:23–27 makes it clear that the chief priests' response to Jesus's question is influenced by the fact that they know the Jews recognize John the Baptist as a prophet.

John was first confirmed as a prophet of God by his miraculous arrival. Luke 1 records that his father, Zechariah, received a message from the angel Gabriel that his wife, who was beyond childbearing age, would give birth to a son. Later John fulfills the role of the prophet spoken of in Isaiah 40:3–5 as the one who prepares the way for the Messiah. His preaching is empowered by the Holy Spirit and moves men and women to repentance and baptism. Jesus reminds the Jewish leaders that they responded positively to John's ministry because they "chose for a time to enjoy his light" (John 5:35). The word *enjoy* denotes an overflowing and enthusiastic happiness.[6] Although these leaders exult in God's gift of a prophet in their generation, ironically, they do not receive his message.

John, a recognized prophet of God, acknowledges that Jesus existed before him—"the Lamb of God, who takes away the sin of the world" (John 1:29)—even though John's physical birth was six months before Jesus's (Luke 1:35–36). He also recognizes the divine nature of Christ, declaring that Jesus "surpassed me because he was before me. . . . I myself did not know him, but the reason I came baptizing with water was that he might be revealed to Israel" (John 1:15, 31).

The Witness of Jesus's Works

The second witness Christ calls to the stand is his works. These works include Jesus's entire ministry.[7] There is probably an emphasis here on his miracles since it was the miracle Jesus just performed (John 5:1–9) that instigated this confrontation. Although the word most often used for miracle is *sign* (*semeion*), Andrew Lincoln sees an overlap in meaning between works referred to here and the miracle signs.[8] For example, in John 6:30 the words *sign* (*semeion*) and *work* (*ergon*) are used interchangeably (NKJV). In John 9:3 the phrase "work of God" refers to the miracle that Jesus is about to perform.

Only God can perform true miracles, and he uses miracles to confirm his message and messengers. Since he is a God of truth, he does not associate his miracles with a false message. Because Christ's miracles are witnessed by multitudes and are therefore undeniable, the Jews have to take into account the testimony of his works. Nicodemus makes the connection when he comes to Jesus at night and says, "Rabbi, we know you are a teacher who has come from God. For no one could perform the miraculous signs you are doing if God were not with him" (John 3:2). Charismatic leaders can gain a following through the power of their speech and personality, but Christ displays more than the ability to stir people's hearts—he demonstrates authority over creation.

The Witness of the Father

The third witness Jesus brings forward is his Father. God the Father possesses the greatest authority, and so his testimony counts the most heavily in this case. Exactly how God has personally testified on behalf of Jesus is not specified. The Greek word for the verb *witness* is in the perfect tense, which indicates the witness took place in the past but has continuing significance.[9] Some commentators believe John could be referring to Jesus's baptism when God's voice from heaven confirmed Jesus (Mark 1:11). Although this event is not recorded in John's Gospel, we can assume John and his readers are familiar with it. Other commentators suppose this refers to the testimony of the Holy Spirit working in the heart of the believer, using 1 John 5:9–10 to support this interpretation.

D. A. Carson offers another good explanation. The testimony Jesus refers to is a general reference to the Father's revealing work in the life of Christ: the testimony of Scripture, special events such as baptism, the confirming work of the Spirit in those who recognize the true nature of Christ, and the later work of redemption.[10] All these revelations are from the Father, who testifies on behalf of his Son.

The Witness of Scripture

The fourth witness Christ presents is the Old Testament Scriptures. Jesus rebukes the Jewish leaders, who "diligently study the

Scriptures" but fail to understand its true content and purpose (John 5:39). The prophecies, typologies, and symbols point to Jesus Christ, and he states in Matthew 5:17 that he came to fulfill the Law and the Prophets.

The reason these leaders fail to recognize Jesus as the Messiah is revealed in the following verses of John 5. These men do not have the love of God in them, and they are seeking the praise of one another rather than the praise of God. This is in contrast to Jesus, who does not seek the praise of humans (vv. 41–44).

At this point in the dialogue, Jesus begins to turn the tables on his accusers, and the defendant now becomes the prosecutor. The Jewish leaders' façade is exposed, showing that their true intent and motivation for accusing Jesus is not that they are concerned for God's glory but that they are seeking the praise of people. If they truly loved God, they would love the one whom God sent, who performs works in perfect harmony with the will of God.[11]

The Witness of Moses

Finally, Jesus turns the table on the Jews in John 5:45–47. He appeals to Moses, the greatest Old Testament prophet, as his witness. In his stern rebuke, Jesus states that he will not be the one accusing the Jews on the last day; instead their accuser will be Moses, the prophet they greatly esteem. The irony is evident: Moses, who is viewed as the great advocate of the Jews (Job 1:20; T. Mos. 11:17; As. Mos. 12:6), now becomes their prosecutor.[12]

Jesus does not point out a specific passage here, but Moses was the author of the Old Testament law, and the Jews place their trust in his writings. The Jewish leaders base their salvation on obedience to the law, but they fail to understand its true meaning. The law is not the end in itself; it is a witness to Jesus Christ. These Jews place their hope in Moses but not in the one about whom he wrote. The words of Moses and Jesus are connected to one another: to believe one is to believe the other; to reject one is to reject the other. Moses wrote the law; Jesus came to fulfill the law (Matt. 5:17).[13]

Given that the law only required two or three witnesses, Jesus could not be required to provide the Jews with a greater number of witnesses for his claims. Further, in the Judaistic context, Jesus provides the greatest possible witnesses: the greatest prophet (John the Baptist), the greatest works (miracles), the greatest being (God), the greatest book (the Torah), and the greatest lawgiver (Moses). Any unbiased Jewish jury would have been overwhelmed by the evidence.

Jesus's Use of a Fourfold Apologetic Testimony

A similar confrontation is recorded in John 8. Jesus claims, "I am the light of the world. Whoever follows me will never walk in darkness, but will have the light of life" (John 8:12). At this the Pharisees are angered and dismiss Jesus's words because he is testifying on his own behalf (v. 13).

The Self-Testimony of the Son

Jesus responds that his testimony is validated by his knowledge of his origin and future destination. He affirms, "Even if I bear witness of Myself, My witness is true, for I know where I came from and where I am going" (John 8:14 NKJV). That is, Jesus as God incarnate is the highest authority and needs no one to validate his claim.

The Testimony of the Father

Jesus then caters to the Jewish law and states, as in Matthew 5:17–20, that the Father testifies on his behalf. The reason the Pharisees do not know Jesus is that they do not know God. This is similar to the indictment in verse 17, where Jesus says, in effect, that not only is his testimony of the Father valid because he is God's Son, but also the Father testifies to the same fact, namely, that Jesus is his Son. In Jesus's words, "If you had known Me, you would have known My Father also" (John 8:19 NKJV).

The Testimony of Abraham

Other than Moses, no Old Testament figure is more revered by the Jews than Abraham. Indeed, the Jews call themselves the children of Abraham. So Jesus turns the tables by stating that if they know Abraham, are the true children of Abraham, and trust in the God whom Abraham trusted, they will recognize Jesus and receive him. By calling upon Abraham, Jesus plays his *ace* witness. The father of the Jews rejoices to see Christ (John 8:56), so if these Jews are the sons of Abraham, they would receive him as Abraham did. Their response reveals they do not believe in the God of the one they claim as their ancestor.

The Testimony of a Sinless Life

Cut to the heart by the irrefutable logic of Jesus, the Jews turn to ad hominem arguments: "We were not born of fornication," and later, "Now we know that You have a demon." Jesus's answer is straight and to the point: "Which of you convicts Me of sin?" (John 8:41, 46, 52 NKJV). In short, the evidence for Jesus's impeccable life demonstrates that his testimony is true. Indeed, there are shadows here of the famous trilemma: Either Christ is a liar, a lunatic, or Lord. But if he is not a liar (for which they have no evidence), then he is either a lunatic or Lord. But how could he be a lunatic since he has God, Abraham, and his own sinless life as his witnesses?

Some, like Bertrand Russell, have searched for flaws in Jesus's character, but their efforts have proved futile. Russell argues that anyone who warns people of eternal punishment is not "profoundly humane."[14] But this begs the question of whether there is a hell, for if there is a hell—and Jesus as the Son of God should know—then it would be profoundly inhumane *not* to warn people that they are headed there! Russell's other argument—that anyone who unnecessarily drowns pigs, as Jesus did, is unkind—fares no better. One could say that Russell's argument is overconfident and based on a lack of knowledge. First of all, Jesus did not drown the pigs; the demons did. Second, Jesus is master of his creation and therefore can do what he wills with those he has created. Third, Russell is more interested in the pigs than the people whom Jesus delivered from the demons. The character of Christ has been well attested by both friend and foe.[15] Indeed, Russell himself says that even though Christ is not perfect (based on his imperfect arguments above), nonetheless, "I grant Him a very high degree of moral goodness."[16] He also says elsewhere that what the world needs is "love, Christian love, or compassion"[17]— which is a great compliment to the character of Christ. Indeed, no one has expressed any greater love than Christ (John 15:13; Rom. 5:6–8). Brilliant as Russell is, a careful analysis reveals that the flaws are not in Christ's character but in Russell's arguments.

Conclusion

From these examples of Jesus, we learn several key lessons: First, in making his case, Jesus gives reasons and evidence for his claims. He does not expect his listeners simply to believe or make a blind leap of faith. Second, the evidence Jesus gives includes firsthand, eyewitness, and supernatural events. Third, Jesus provides multiple witnesses in defense of his claim. This is a key part of Jesus's apologetics, which includes testimony from credible witnesses. Thus, given his monotheistic context, Jesus is an evidentialist, not a fideist, in that he believes in the use of evidence to convince others of the truth of his claims.

In John 5:31–47 Jesus presents five credible witnesses: John the Baptist, his works, the Father, the Old Testament, and Moses. In John 8:12–41 Jesus points to the testimony of his heavenly Father and adds the testimony of Abraham and of his own sinless life. The power of Jesus's argument rests in the integrity and credibility of his witnesses. Not only does he present forceful witnesses, but in the process of defending himself, he turns the tables on his accusers. No reasonable Jew has any valid grounds on which to reject Jesus's witnesses; his apologetic tactic is very effective.

2

Jesus's
Apologetic Use of
Miracles

Anyone who claims to be God in human flesh needs to offer sufficient validations if he expects people to believe him. This is exactly what Jesus does. A key component of Christ's apologetic is the miraculous signs that he performs to substantiate his claim. The monotheistic Jews to whom Jesus speaks understand this. The Jewish Pharisee Nicodemus says, "Rabbi, we know that You are a teacher come from God; for no one can do these signs [miracles] that You do unless God is with him" (John 3:2 NKJV). It was customary for God to validate his spokesperson in this way—for example, Moses (Exod. 4:1–17) and Elijah (1 Kings 18). Indeed, the Jews of Jesus's day were seeking a sign from God (Matt. 12:39).

There are several key periods in which miracles occurred more regularly. The first was the Mosaic period. At that time God was establishing the authority of his messenger, Moses, and the authority of the law. The second age of miracles was the prophetic period. This began with Elijah and Elisha. At that time God was reestablishing his law after Israel fell into national apostasy and rebelled against the authority of the prophets. Later, the prophet Daniel manifested a continuance of miracles as God preserved his people in exile, proclaimed his glory to foreign nations, and gave Daniel a prophetic message of future events. The fourth period of miracles was during apostolic times. This began with Christ, who was established and confirmed through miracles as God's Son, the Messiah of Israel.

In each age, miracles were used to confirm God's message through his messengers. The writer of Hebrews declares, "How shall we escape if we neglect so great a salvation, which at the first began to be spoken by the Lord, and was confirmed to us by those who heard Him [the apostles], God also bearing witness both with signs and wonders, with various miracles, and gifts of the Holy Spirit, according to His own will" (Heb. 2:3–4 NKJV). Craig Blomberg states, "The purpose of Jesus' miracle-working ministry has been described as 'evidential, evangelistic, empathetic, and eschatological.' . . . But the primary focus is Christological—to demonstrate that Jesus is the divine Messiah and that the kingdom of God is now breaking into human history with new force (Matt. 11:2–6, Luke 11:20)."[1]

In Deuteronomy 18:14–20 God promises that he will one day raise another prophet like Moses through whom he will speak. The miracles of Christ are signs that he is that prophet and more. Although many Jews who see the signs are convinced, not everyone makes the connection.

In John 2:1–11 it is Jesus's miraculous work of turning water into wine that causes his disciples to place their faith in him. "This, the first of his miraculous signs, Jesus performed in Cana of Galilee. He thus revealed his glory, and his disciples put their faith in him" (v. 11). The Jewish leader Nicodemus also recognizes his miracles as a confirmation that Jesus is sent from God (John 3:2).

Miracles Defined

Natural laws describe what occurs regularly by natural causes, but miracles are special acts of God that interrupt the normal course of events and confirm the Word of God through a messenger of God.[2]

Several words are used for *miracle* in the Gospels. Dwight Pentecost defines the terms used in the New Testament.

1. *Teras* occurs sixteen times in the New Testament and is always used in combination with *semeion* (signs). It stresses the startling, imposing, and amazing aspect of the miracle.
2. *Dynamis* emphasizes the power revealed in the miracle and the spiritual energy behind it.
3. *Endoxos* emphasizes miracles as being works in which the glory of God and the Son are revealed.
4. *Paradoxos* is used only in Luke 5:26, and it is translated "remarkable things." It emphasizes that the miracle is contrary to the natural order of the world.
5. *Thaumasios* is used only in Matthew 21:15 and means something that provokes wonder.
6. *Semeion* is used to point to the power or meaning behind the miracle.[3]

The Greek word most often used is *semeion* (usually translated "sign"). It appears seventy-seven times in the New Testament, primarily in the Gospels, where it is used forty-eight times. The basic meaning of *semeion* is a sign by which one recognizes a particular person or thing and which serves as an authenticating mark or token. When associated with the miraculous, it can indicate a miracle accomplished by a divinity or miracle worker that goes against the natural course of things.[4] The other Greek terms used for *miracle* lead us to conclude that miracles are unique and extraordinary events awakening wonder (*teras*), brought about by divine power (*dynamis*), accomplishing some practical and benevolent work (*ergon* and *endoxos*), and authenticating the message and messenger as coming from God (*semeion*).[5]

There is greater meaning to miracles, however, than just the events themselves. There are at least five dimensions to biblical miracles that can be listed:

1. Miracles have an unusual character; as a wonder, they attract attention.
2. Miracles have a theological dimension. God, who created and sustains the universe, can intervene whenever he chooses.
3. There is a moral dimension to miracles. They reflect the character of God and bring glory to him.
4. Miracles have a doctrinal dimension. They are often connected to truth claims and confirm God's message and messenger.
5. Miracles have a teleological dimension. They are never performed to entertain but rather to glorify God and provide evidence to cause people to believe that God's authority is upon the messenger.[6]

The Jews understood that only God could perform true miracles (see Exod. 8:19). Since God does not associate with false teachings, Christ cannot perform miracles if his claims are false. Therefore, his miracles validate Jesus's extraordinary claim to be the divine Son of God, the Messiah. They also provoke a response from those who witness them. The proper conclusion the Jews should have come to after seeing Jesus's miracles is that someone with the authority of God has come to initiate the coming of the kingdom of God.

Satan and Miracles

Some have argued that Satan can also perform miracles (Matt. 7:22–23; 2 Thess. 2:9). But Satan, being a finite creature, is unable to perform truly supernatural acts as God does, for only a supernatural being (God) can perform supernatural acts. For example, Satan is unable to create life or resurrect someone from the dead. If Satan possesses the power to raise the dead, this would present a serious problem for using the resurrection of Jesus Christ to confirm his deity. Some have used Revelation 13 to support the contrary view; however, careful examination reveals the contrary.

In Revelation 13 the Antichrist is fatally wounded and then is miraculously healed of his wound (vv. 3, 12). Some believe that the

Antichrist is killed and then is raised to life by Satan. Tim LaHaye presents this scenario in his endtimes fiction series.[7] But the New International Version translates verse 3: "One of the heads of the beast seemed to have had a fatal wound, but the fatal wound had been healed." The Greek reads, *hos esphagmenen eis thanaton*. New Testament scholar Leon Morris states that this may be translated "as though slain."[8] Therefore, we can conclude that the Beast is not really killed but is seriously wounded and near death. He is then healed from this wound but not resurrected from the dead.

Revelation 13:15 states that the Beast "was given power to give breath to the image of the first beast, so that it could speak." Some believe that Satan demonstrates the power to create life in this passage. First of all, whatever power the Beast has is given to him by God. So the source of this "breath" or "life" does not originate with Satan but is granted to him by God. Further, the word *breath* is a translation of the Greek word *pneuma*. Some translate this word as "life," but the New International Version says "breath," which is a more accurate translation. *Pneuma* is quite different from the Greek word for *life*, which is *zoe*. The image is not given life but breath, which could indicate that the image has the appearance of life. John Walvoord states, "The intent of the passage seems to be that the image has the appearance of life manifested in breathing, but actually it may be no more than a robot. The image is further described being able to speak, a faculty easily accomplished by mechanical means."[9] There are numerous scenarios that provide reasonable explanations for how the image appears to receive a lifelike appearance.

So neither passage provides any real support for the view that Satan can resurrect the dead. The whole of Scripture speaks against it, for everywhere God alone is presented as the Creator of "every living thing" (Gen. 1:21 NKJV). Indeed, God himself says, "I, even I, am He, and there is no God besides me; I kill and I make alive" (Deut. 32:39 NKJV; cf. Job 1:21). Even the magicians of Egypt acknowledge that only God could create life out of dust, for they say of Moses's miracle, "This is the finger of God" (Exod. 8:19). To claim that Satan can do miracles on a par with God's supernatural acts to create life or raise the dead is to destroy the whole apologetic foundation on which Christianity rests (1 Cor. 15:12–19). Satan is a master magician and a superscientist. He does many things that look like miracles, but the Bible calls them "lying wonders" or "false signs" (2 Thess. 2:9 NKJV). Only God has the ability to perform a truly supernatural act. Satan is a finite creature, and as such he cannot match the infinite power of God. Hence, Christ's miracles are unique.

Christ's Miracles and Mystery Religions

Others attempt to diminish the unique apologetic value of Christ's miracles by claiming they originate in mystery religions. But this view is without foundation for many reasons.

First, the view involves the composite fallacy. When making comparisons to Christianity, proponents lump together pagan religions as if they are one. By combining features from various religions, an attempt is made to show strong parallels.[10] When the individual myths themselves are studied, however, the reader discovers major differences with very little commonality.

Second, it entails the fallacy of terminology. Christian terms are also used to describe pagan beliefs, so it is concluded that there are parallel origins and meanings. But even though the words used are the same, there is a big difference between the Christian practice and definition and the pagan understanding.[11]

Third is the chronological fallacy. Supporters of this position incorrectly assume that Christianity borrowed many of its ideas from the mystery religions, when the evidence reveals it was actually the other way around. There is no archaeological evidence that mystery religions existed in Israel in the first century AD. Jews and early Christians loathed syncretism and were uncompromisingly monotheistic, while Greeks were polytheistic. Christians also strongly defended the uniqueness of Christ as the only Son of God and the only way to eternal life (Acts 4:12). Although Christians encountered pagan religions, they opposed adopting any foreign beliefs.[12] Ron Nash states, "The uncompromising monotheism and the exclusiveness that the early church preached and practiced make the possibility of any pagan inroads . . . unlikely if not impossible."[13]

Fourth is the intentional fallacy. Christianity has a linear view that there is a reason for mankind's existence and that history is moving in a purposeful direction to fulfill God's plan for the ages. The mystery religions have a cyclical view of history, believing that history continues in a never-ending cycle that is often linked with the vegetation cycle.[14]

In short, Christianity finds its source in Judaism, not Greek mythology. Jesus, Paul, and the apostles appeal to the Old Testament, where we find prophecies that Christianity fulfills. Old Testament teachings such as one God, blood atonement for sin, salvation by grace, sinfulness of humankind, and bodily resurrection find their source in Judaism and are foreign to Greek mythology. The idea of resurrection was not taught in any Greek mythological work prior to the late second century AD.[15] Jesus's miracles are not mythological literary replicas; they are unique supernatural events.

Authority Demonstrated in Jesus's Miraculous Signs

Throughout the Old Testament, God used miracles to confirm his message and his messenger. Christ's miracles demonstrated that what he claimed about himself was true and that God's confirming hand was on the message he preached. Jesus performed a vast array of miraculous signs that demonstrated him to be God incarnate and confirmed his authority over every realm of creation.

Jesus's power over the cosmos was manifested by his control over every category of the cosmos, as listed by the famous Greek philosopher Aristotle in his *Categories*. Note Jesus's power over:

- Substance (What?)—Turning water into wine
- Quantity (How much?)—Feeding five thousand
- Quality (What kind?)—Blind man gets the quality known as sight
- Relation (To what?)—Raising Lazarus to his relationship with others living

- Space (Where?)—Healing nobleman's son from a distance
- Time (When?)—Healing an invalid of thirty-eight years
- Position (On what?)—Walking on water, an unnatural position
- Action (From what?)—His Victorious Death
- Passion (On what?)—His Triumphant Resurrection
- State or Habit (Under what condition?)—Catching an over-abundance of fish[16]

The miracles of Christ reflect his divine character and demonstrate his authority over creation. When he establishes his kingdom on earth, all creation will be subject to him. Sin, sickness, death, and disease will ultimately be overcome (1 Cor. 15:20–26; Rev. 21:4), and the subjects of his kingdom will never be in want. The King will supply all their needs.

Jesus performs several miracles that demonstrate his supernatural knowledge. In the calling of Nathanael (John 1:43–51), Christ reveals his knowledge of Nathanael's location and even his thoughts. As a result, Nathanael exclaims, "Rabbi, you are the Son of God; you are the King of Israel" (John 1:49). In John 4:1–38 Jesus reveals his knowledge of the Samaritan woman's life when he says that she had five previous husbands and is presently living with a man who is not her husband. As a result, she reports to her fellow townspeople, "Come, see a man who told me everything I ever did. Could this be the Christ?" (v. 29). Jesus's special knowledge of individuals and events demonstrates that he is capable of exercising his divine attribute of omniscience.

Jesus demonstrates that as Creator he has authority over the natural world. Examples of this authority are seen when he calms the storm (Luke 8:22–25), transforms water into wine (John 2:1–11), and walks on water (John 6:16–24). As Jehovah the healer, Christ demonstrates authority over disease. He cures leprosy (Matt. 8:1–4), blindness (Mark 10:46–52; John 9:1–12), sickness (John 4:43–54), and physical infirmities (John 5:1–15).

As Lord over all creation, Christ's authority extends even over the spiritual realm. He demonstrates power over demonic forces by exorcising them from two men in the region of the Gadarenes (Matt. 8:28–34), from a boy with an evil spirit (Mark 9:14–32; Luke 9:37–45), and from the Gerasene demoniac (Luke 8:26–39).

As Yahweh the provider, Jesus demonstrates his ability to provide for the people's needs. He feeds a crowd of five thousand (Matt. 14:13–21) and later a crowd of four thousand (Matt. 15:29–39). In Luke 5:1–11, Jesus performs the miracle of the miraculous catch of fish. The provision of food parallels God providing for his people during the exodus from Egypt.

Jesus shows his authority over sin and its effects in Mark 2:1–12. Upon seeing the paralytic lowered before him, Jesus declares to the man, "Son, your sins are forgiven" (v. 5). The Jewish leaders hearing this are offended because they know only God has the authority to forgive sins, which means Jesus is claiming to exercise the authority reserved for God. Knowing their thoughts, Jesus responds, "'But that you may know that the Son of Man has authority on earth to forgive sins. . . .' He said to the paralytic, 'I tell you, get up, take your mat and go home'" (vv. 10–11). Thus, Jesus presents a physical demonstration to the audience of his authority over sin.

Jesus is also the source of life. He demonstrates this by raising several people from the dead. They include Jairus's daughter (Mark 5:21–24, 35–43), the widow's son in the town of Nain (Luke 7:11–17), and Lazarus (John 11).

Through this wide variety of miracles, Jesus demonstrates his authority over every realm of creation. The vast array of Christ's miracles confirms he is "the image of the invisible God, the firstborn over all creation" (Col. 1:15). In short, miracles are used repeatedly as Christ's apologetic to confirm and defend his message.

The Apologetic of Miracles

Jesus is often called upon to defend his claims. When this happens, he points people to the testimony of his miracles. In John 10 the

Jews challenge Jesus, "How long will you keep us in suspense? If you are the Christ, tell us plainly" (v. 24). In response to this challenge to substantiate his claim, Jesus points his opponents to the clear and vivid testimony of his miracles: "I did tell you, but you do not believe. The miracles I do in my Father's name speak for me" (v. 25). D. A. Carson states, "The array of his deeds—including the restoration of a man paralyzed for thirty-eight years, the thoroughly attested healing of a man born blind, and, shortly, the resurrection of a man indisputably dead—along with the tone and content of his teaching, speak volumes on his behalf."[17] To a very hardened group who demand convincing evidence, Jesus points to his miracles. The connection between Jesus, the truth of his message, and God's authority is obvious.

The passage in John 10 goes on to state that the Jews pick up stones to stone Jesus. As his defense, Jesus again appeals to the testimony of his miracles, which are the work of God: "I have shown you many great miracles from the Father. For which of these do you stone me?" (v. 32). Then he presents an a fortiori argument from Psalm 82:6.

> Is it not written in your Law, "I have said you are gods"? If he called them "gods," to whom the word of God came—and the Scripture cannot be broken—what about the one whom the Father set apart as his very own and sent into the world? Why then do you accuse me of blasphemy because I said, "I am God's Son"?
>
> John 10:34–36

Then Jesus appeals a third time to the evidence of his miracles: "Even though you do not believe me, believe the miracles, that you may know and understand that the Father is in me, and I in the Father" (v. 38). Jesus does not expect the crowd to believe based on his words alone. He points to the evidence he wants them to seriously consider—his miracles.[18]

Another opportunity arises for Jesus to defend his claims, but this time it is to a friendly crowd. The popular expectation is that the Messiah will initiate the kingdom, which will be characterized by liberty and freedom. But the kingdom does not materialize, and John the Baptist finds himself in prison and in danger of execution. Not knowing what to make of this development, John becomes discouraged and perhaps disillusioned. Questioning his decision regarding Jesus, he sends his disciples to ask, "Are you the one who was to come, or should we expect someone else?" (Matt. 11:3; Luke 7:20). Jesus responds by pointing to the testimony of his miracles: "Go back and report to John what you hear and see: The blind receive sight, the lame walk, those who have leprosy are cured, the deaf hear, the dead are raised, and the good news is preached to the poor" (Matt. 11:4–5; see also Luke 7:22). Jesus gives a summary of his works, referencing Isaiah 35:4–6 and 61:1. He assures John that the messianic visions of these passages are being fulfilled. The proof is demonstrated in the miracles of Christ and the preaching of the gospel to the poor. The powers of darkness are being dismantled as the King begins ushering in the kingdom.[19] Knowing John's doubts and situation, he points to the compelling testimony of his miracles and his works in order to not leave the prophet with any questions in his mind.

The Uniqueness of Christ's Miracles

Jesus's miracles confirm his claim to be the divine Son of God, demonstrate his authority over every realm of creation, and set him apart from the founders of all other religions. Most of the miracle accounts from other religions are mythical and were written down several generations after the lifetime of the eyewitnesses. Historian A. N. Sherwin White documents that it takes at least two to three generations after the death of the eyewitnesses for complete legends to develop.[20] William Lane Craig states, "The writings of the Greek historian Herodotus enable us to test the rate at which a legend accumulates; the tests show that even the span of two generations is too short to allow legendary tendencies to wipe out the hard core of historical fact."[21] Since the Gospels were written in the generation of the eyewitnesses, it was too early for a full legend to develop.

In contrast to other ancient miracle claims, the New Testament provides written accounts of the events of Jesus's life accurately recorded by multiple eyewitnesses and close associates of Christ. Their testimony and writings were circulating within the lifetime of other eyewitnesses and in the cities where these events occurred. As we have seen (in chap. 1), *witness* is a pivotal concept in John's Gospel, and the reason for this is clear: the signs Jesus performed are thoroughly attested by many witnesses; therefore, these miracles cannot be simply dismissed or explained away.

Many of the eyewitnesses were hostile and looking for a way to discredit the historical veracity of the message of the apostles. If Jesus's miracles were fictional, the hostile eyewitnesses could have easily discredited the Gospels and the testimony of the disciples, who pointed to the miracles of Christ as an apologetic for their message. In other words, Christianity could not have lasted if the miracle accounts of Jesus were not true.

In contrast to the historical nature of Christ's miracles, accounts from other religions of miracles are often mythical in nature. The Gnostic gospels are a clear example of this. For instance, *The Gospel of Peter* says that the cross upon which Christ was crucified walked and talked at the resurrection. Then it states that the necks of the angels at the tomb stretched to the heavens and the neck of Christ stretched beyond the heavens. Few take this to be a historical account of the resurrection.

The majority of miracle claims from other religions were written at least two generations after the lifetime of the eyewitnesses and, therefore, are not first-generation historical accounts as are the Christian Gospels. The Qu'ran does not attribute any miracles to Muhammad; in fact, he refuses to do so (Sura 28:47–51). Muslims claim, however, that he did many miracles, referencing the *Hadith*, which records the alleged sayings of Muhammad. But this work was written at least a century after the lifetime of Muhammad.[22] The *Hadith* as well as the Gnostic gospels follow this pattern of legendary miracle accounts that began to develop two generations later. Further, there is evidence they were created in order to answer

Christian apologists who appealed to Christ's miracles as evidence that his claims to be God were supernaturally confirmed, as opposed to Muhammad, who did no such miracles.

One Final Miraculous Sign

The miracles of Christ brought many to faith (see chap. 3), but the resurrection was the greatest miracle of all. Despite his numerous miracles, many still refused to believe. John writes, "Even after Jesus had done all these miraculous signs in their presence, they still would not believe in him" (John 12:37). After he clears the temple, the Jews challenge Jesus to perform another sign to prove his authority to do such things. Jesus refuses to do another miracle at that moment because of the hardness of their hearts, but he says a final sign will be given: "Destroy this temple, and I will raise it again in three days" (John 2:19). The Jews, failing to grasp what he means, reply, "It has taken forty-six years to build this temple, and you are going to raise it in three days?" (John 2:20). They do not understand that the temple he is speaking of is his body. After Jesus's resurrection, his disciples remember and understand, and this also convinces some of the most skeptical Jews (see, for example, John 12:42; Acts 9).

On another occasion the Pharisees and teachers of the law demand a sign from Jesus. Knowing they are making an insincere request, he replies, "A wicked and adulterous generation asks for a miraculous sign! But none will be given it except the sign of the prophet Jonah. For as Jonah was three days and three nights in the belly of a huge fish, so the Son of Man will be three days and three nights in the heart of the earth" (Matt. 12:39–40).

Application for Apologetics Today

In the monotheistic context to which Jesus speaks, a miracle is the greatest evidence that can be given, for if God exists, then miracles are possible, and God uses miracles to confirm his message from his spokespersons (Acts 2:22; Heb. 2:3–4). Therefore, the truth of Jesus's claims are established by miracles. They are acts of God to confirm his truth through his messengers to the people of God.

Miracles are strong evidence in building a case for Christianity. Jesus uses miracles to demonstrate the truth of his claims—they are a clear sign that he is God incarnate. And when his opponents question him, he points to those miracles as authentication of his claims to be the divine Son of God (see Mark 2:8–12).

In presenting the case for Christianity, apologists today can utilize this same miraculous evidence. Of course, current apologists have the added burden of showing that the New Testament documents are historically reliable, which they can readily do.[23] The miracles of Christ set him apart from leaders of other religions and demonstrate his authority over every realm of creation. Of all the claims of world religious leaders, only those of Christ are uniquely verified by multiple, repeated, eyewitness testimony.

Arguments against Christ's Miracles

The most formidable arguments against miracles are from David Hume. His arguments, or modified versions of them, are still used today to argue against the miracle accounts of Christ. Hume believes that Christianity cannot be true because miracles are impossible. Since it uses the testimony of miracles to substantiate its claims to be the true faith, Christianity builds its claims on a false premise. Regarding his argument Hume states, "I flatter myself that I have discovered an argument . . . which, if just, will, with the wise and learned, be an everlasting check to all kinds of superstitious delusion, and consequently will be useful as long as the world endures."[24]

Hume's Presupposition

Hume's argument is built on his belief in a naturalistic universe in which the laws of the universe cannot be altered and there is no God who can intervene. Since most of those to whom Jesus ministered were monotheists, he had no need to provide theistic evidence for them. If there had been such occasions, he readily could have appealed to the design of the heavens (Ps. 19:1) or the need for a Creator of the world (Acts 14:15–17; 17:24–28; Rom. 1:19–20). Indeed, there is strong evidence that indicates that we live in a theistic universe. Following is a brief summary of the evidence for the existence of God.

First, there is the argument from *first cause*, also known as the *cosmological argument*, which states that whatever begins to exist had a cause. The scientific evidence shows that the universe has a beginning, and therefore it must have had a cause. It is illogical to assume that nothing created the universe, for it is impossible for the universe to be produced from nothing. There must have been someone or something greater than the universe to create it. Such a *first cause* is what we call God: a supernatural being beyond the natural universe who brought it into existence. The scientific evidence that the universe had a beginning is overwhelming. It includes the second law of thermodynamics, the expanding universe, the radiation afterglow, Einstein's general theory of relativity, and the great mass of energy discovered by the Hubble space telescope—all of which point to a beginning of the space-time universe.[25] In view of this evidence, even agnostic astronomer Robert Jastrow confesses, "That there are what I or anyone would call supernatural forces at work is now, I think, a scientifically proven fact."[26]

Second, the apparent order and design in nature points to an intelligent designer. For example, none of us would assume that a computer is produced as the result of natural forces. Although all the components of a computer can be found on earth, we would never assume that wind, rain, and lightning somehow produced something as complex and sophisticated as a computer. If we can arrive at that conclusion, how much more can we similarly deduce that the human brain, which is even more complex than a computer, did not randomly come into being? Apparent design can be found in all arenas of creation. Scientists such as Michael Behe and Bill Dembsky have shown in their books that throughout the universe we find specified complexity and irreducible complexity. The incredible design of the universe points to an intelligent designer.[27]

Third, verification of the existence of God is our moral intuition. We inherently know right from wrong. All people recognize that it is wrong to torture and murder a child for entertainment. All people acknowledge that rape is wrong. This universal moral law embedded in the hearts of humans points to a moral lawgiver who established a moral law code and placed it in the conscience of every person. This moral lawgiver is God. Former atheist C. S. Lewis forcefully presents this argument in his famous book *Mere Christianity*.[28]

If a theistic God exists, then miracles are not only possible but also actual. This is exemplified by the fact that the greatest miracle occurred when God created the universe out of nothing. If there is a God who acts, then there can be acts of God.[29] Moreover, if this miracle has already taken place, it is also reasonable to ask, When else has God acted in human history? The existence of God dismantles the foundational premise of Hume's argument.

Hume's Argument against Miracles

Hume's argument against miracles is summarized as follows.

1. A miracle is by definition a rare occurrence.
2. Natural law is by definition a description of regular occurrence.
3. Evidence for the regular is always greater than for the rare.
4. Wise individuals always base belief on the greater evidence.
5. Therefore, wise individuals should never believe in miracles.[30]

Hume's first and second premises are valid; however, point three is not. The evidence for the regular is not always greater than for the rare. Hume's mistake here is that he adds up the evidence against miracles but does not weigh the evidence. He assumes that since natural laws are rarely or never violated, one should assume naturalistic explanations and not consider the possibility that a rare event (such as a miracle) has occurred. So his position is that a rare event can never have as much evidence as common events. Although Hume's conclusion is true most of the time, there are times when the evidence that a rare event has occurred is greater.

For example, if someone falls four hundred feet off a rocky cliff, the vast majority of the time he or she will die. There is the possibility, however, that a rare event could happen and the person might survive such a fall. In fact, I knew a young man in high school who fell off a four-hundred-foot rocky cliff and survived; he is now an evangelist. According to Hume, we should not believe this man survived, because it is a rare event. But here the evidence for a rare event outweighs the evidence for the norm because there were numerous eyewitnesses and written accounts. Rather than examining the evidence for a miracle account, Hume simply assumes the higher probability for a common event to occur outweighs the evidence for rare events such as miracles. But a wise person will examine the evidence and not just assume all experience is uniform. Thus, Hume's argument against miracles fails.

Hume's Argument of Self-Canceling Claims

Hume's second argument against miracles is that all religions use miracles to support their system, and since these religious systems are contrary to each other, no miracle can be used to support any of them. (Contraries cannot be true; they cancel each other out.) His argument can be summarized as follows:

1. Many religious systems use miracles to support their claims.
2. But these religions hold contrary truth claims that can't be true.
3. Therefore, no miracle can be used to support a religious system.[31]

This argument fails, however, because Hume falsely assumes all alleged miracle claims from all the religions are equal. But not all religions have eyewitness accounts like Christianity. For example, the Qu'ran does not include accounts of any miracles performed by the prophet Muhammad,[32] and the miracle accounts in the *Hadith* were recorded over one hundred years after Muhammad lived. In contrast, the miracles of Christ are attested to by people who preached, taught, and wrote down their accounts in the generation of the eyewitnesses.

In addition, not all religions have reliable manuscript evidence. The New Testament has thousands of ancient manuscripts—5,700 Greek manuscripts, some of which date as early as the second century AD. If we include the early translations of these manuscripts, we have over 24,000 manuscripts. There are also over 36,000 quotations of these manuscripts (including all but eleven verses) from the early church fathers, who wrote in the late first and early second centuries. Finally, the writings of non-Christians such as Thallus and Josephus corroborate the basic events of the life of Christ as recorded in the Gospels. The abundant evidence shows that the multiple eyewitness accounts were accurately preserved.

Hume's Argument Regarding the Absence of Credible Witnesses

Hume says, "There is not to be found, in all history, any miracle attested by a sufficient number of men of such unquestioned good-sense, education, and learning as to secure us against all delusion in themselves." Nor are there enough witnesses of "such undoubted integrity, as to place them beyond all suspicion of any design to deceive others." Neither are they "of such credit and reputation in the eyes of mankind, as to have a great deal to lose in case of their being detected in any falsehood."[33]

Hume's third argument is that in fact there never have been a sufficient number of educated people with enough integrity to prove there is no deception and protect us from delusion regarding miracles. The proven tendency of humans, against all probability, to readily believe the miraculous and the many actual forgeries argues against miracles. Also, miracles abound chiefly among the uneducated and the uncultured.

In regard to the Gospel accounts of miracles, Hume states: (1) The people were ignorant. (2) The accounts were recorded long after the event. (3) There was no corroborative or concurring testimony. (4) They resemble fabulous accounts every people have of their origins.

Several historical facts refute Hume's argument: (1) Christianity had educated witnesses such as Paul and Luke. (2) It is wrong to assume that common people cannot be reliable eyewitnesses. (3) There were over five hundred eyewitnesses to the miracles of Christ and the resurrection (as Paul mentions in 1 Cor. 15:6). Not only were there numerous eyewitnesses, but they were also persons of integrity, which is evidenced by the facts that they even recorded their mistakes in their accounts, they did not profit from their message, and many died for rather than retract their testimony. So even according to Hume's criteria, the New Testament witnesses are credible.

The apostles had integrity; they taught their message, lived it, and died for it. Their accounts were recorded in the lifetime of the eyewitnesses, and they were preached and circulated not in a distant land but in the cities where the events had occurred. Finally, there are non-Christian Roman and Jewish sources that corroborate many facts recorded in the Gospels. So Hume's arguments do not invalidate the testimony of miracles remains as valid evidence for the truth of Christianity. Jesus used it to support his deity, and the historical evidence supports his claim.

Conclusion

A miracle is the crowning confirmation of a truth claim made in the name of God. It is a special act of God that confirms a prophet's claim to be speaking the truth of God to the people of God. This was true not only of Old Testament prophets but also of the Messiah they foretold. The miracles of Christ are unique: Not only did he perform many miracles, but there were many witnesses of them. And the nature of many of the miracles he performed placed them beyond reasonable question. He not only cured otherwise incurable diseases, but he also multiplied loaves, walked on water, and raised the dead. These miracles serve as the crowning confirmation of Jesus's truth claims. Along with his resurrection, they provided "many infallible proofs" (Acts 1:3 NKJV) of his claim to deity.

3

Jesus's Apologetic Use of the Resurrection

Jesus confirmed his claims to be the divine Son of God through his miracles (see chap. 2), which demonstrated his authority over every realm of creation. Despite these powerful works, most of the hard-hearted Jewish leaders refused to receive him as their Messiah (John 12:37). To unbelievers such as these, Jesus announced that his final and ultimate sign would be his resurrection from the dead (Matt. 12:40). The resurrection was another major component of his apologetic, and it was central to the teachings of the apostles, who understood that it was the ultimate proof of Christ's deity (1 Cor. 15:12–19).

The hope of everyone who believes in the resurrection and eternal life is built on the historicity of this event. Peter opens his epistle: "All praise to God, the Father of our Lord Jesus Christ. It is by his great mercy that we have been born again, because God raised Jesus Christ from the dead" (1 Peter 1:3 NLT). Our salvation and eternal hope is assured because of the resurrection. Paul states, "If Christ has not been raised, then your faith is useless and you are still guilty of your sins" (1 Cor. 15:17 NLT). Without the resurrection, there is no salvation, and Christianity crumbles. The resurrection affirms that Christ defeated sin and death. It has been part of the Christian's defense of the faith from the beginning and was Christ's apologetic that confirmed the claims he made.

Brief Defense of the Resurrection

Skeptics and opponents of Christianity continue to challenge the historicity of the resurrection. Despite their attacks, the resurrection remains one of the most well-documented ancient historical events. When examining the evidence, we begin by presenting several facts upon which scholars on both sides of the issue agree.

First, Jesus was a prominent figure in Israel, and many people knew his burial site. In fact, Matthew, Mark, and John record the exact location of his tomb. Matthew writes, "A rich man from Arimathea, named Joseph, . . . took the body and wrapped it in a clean linen cloth and laid it in his own new tomb" (Matt. 27:57, 59–60 NRSV). Mark asserts that Joseph was a "prominent member of the [ruling] Council" (Mark 15:43). It would have been destructive for the writers to invent a man of such prominence, name him specifically, and designate the tomb site, since eyewitnesses could have easily discredited the author's false claims.

Both Jewish and Roman sources testify that the tomb was found empty on the third day after Jesus's crucifixion. Matthew 28:12–13 specifically states that the chief priests invented the story that the disciples stole the body. There would be no need for this fabrication if the tomb had not been empty. And the preaching of the apostles would not have lasted if the tomb had not been empty, because the Jewish authorities could have easily put an end to Christianity by producing Jesus's body. But not one historical record from the first or second century attacks the factuality of the empty tomb or claims that Jesus's corpse had been discovered. Opponents of the resurrection must account for this.

Tom Anderson, former president of the California Trial Lawyers Association, states, "Let's assume that the written accounts of His appearances to hundreds of people are false. I want to pose a question. With an event so well publicized, don't you think that it's reasonable that one historian, one eyewitness, one antagonist would record for all time that he had seen the body? . . . The silence from history is deafening when it comes to the testimony against the resurrection."[1]

Second, we have to account for the changed lives of the apostles. The Gospels record that while Jesus is on trial, the disciples desert him in fear. Just a few days later, however, they suddenly return to Jerusalem and begin preaching that Jesus is the Messiah and that he has risen from the dead. All the disciples know this message will bring them a life of suffering and even death, so what accounts for this sudden transformation? Ten out of the eleven remaining apostles (after Judas's death) are martyred because they believe Jesus rose from the dead, and although John is not martyred, he endures persecution until his death. Something very compelling must have occurred to account for this sudden transformation.

Third, the apostles begin preaching the resurrection in Jerusalem, the city in which Jesus was crucified and which is the most hostile city to their message. Furthermore, all the evidence is there for anyone antagonistic to this message to investigate. Legends take root in foreign lands or at least three generations after the event since it is more difficult to discredit them when eyewitnesses are not present. In this case, however, the preaching occurs in the same city and very shortly after Jesus's crucifixion and resurrection. Every possible fact can be investigated thoroughly.

Fourth, we must account for the massive Jewish societal transformation. Thousands of Jews in Jerusalem suddenly abandon major tenets and practices of their faith and accept Jesus as the Messiah who fulfills the law. Thousands of Jews abandon worship on the Sabbath and begin worshiping on Sunday—the day Christ rose from the grave. Numerous Jews abandon temple sacrifices, believing Christ fulfills the sacrificial laws. What is the best explanation for these significant changes among so many Jews?

Finally, one must account for the origin of the church, which from its very beginning preaches Christ's resurrection. This message could not have lasted if the historicity of the resurrection did not have a strong defense in the face of enemies who were seeking to discredit the message of the disciples and the early church. Anyone studying the resurrection must account for these facts.

Alternative Explanations

Given the historical reliability of the Gospel accounts, none of the alternative accounts of the resurrection of Christ make any sense. All of them deny either that Jesus died or that a few days later he appeared numerous times to numerous people in the same physical body in which he had died. Nonetheless, many critics have questioned these facts, so it is necessary to address their alternative explanations.

The Stolen Body Theory

The oldest explanation is the stolen body theory. This explanation began the day of the resurrection and is still believed by many opponents of Christianity. Matthew 28:12–15 records the genesis of this explanation:

> When the chief priests had met with the elders and devised a plan, they gave the soldiers a large sum of money, telling them, "You are to say, 'His disciples came during the night and stole him away while we were asleep.' If this report gets to the governor, we will satisfy him and keep you out of trouble." So the soldiers took the money and did as they were instructed. And this story has been widely circulated among the Jews to this very day.

Some wonder why Matthew records this and then provides no refutation. No doubt it is because this explanation is so unlikely that he sees no need to do so. The idea that Jesus's body was stolen is highly implausible for several reasons.

1. If the soldiers were sleeping, how did they know it was the disciples who stole the body? And Roman guards were not likely to fall asleep on such an important assignment because there were severe penalties for doing so. If they were not asleep, the disciples would have had to overpower armed soldiers, which is a highly unlikely scenario.
2. Even if the guards were asleep, it would have been physically impossible for the disciples to sneak past the soldiers and then silently move a two-ton stone up an incline. Certainly the guards would have heard something.
3. The tomb was secured with a Roman seal. Anyone who moved the stone would break the seal—an offense punishable by death. The depression and cowardice the disciples had exhibited in the Garden of Gethsemane make it difficult to believe that they would suddenly become brave enough to face a detachment of soldiers, steal the body, and then lie about the resurrection.
4. Jesus's crucifixion made it clear that preaching his message would almost certainly lead to a life of suffering and death. History reveals that men and women will not die for what they know to be a lie. So why would the apostles contrive and then preach a story that was certain to bring them persecution?
5. John records that the grave clothes of Jesus, along with the burial cloth that had been around his head, were found neatly folded (see John 20:3–9). If the disciples stole the body, they would have had to sneak past the guards, roll away the stone, unwrap the body, rewrap it in something else, and neatly fold the headpiece and linen before making their escape. In a robbery such as this, they would have flung the garments down in disorder and fled quickly in fear of detection.

All these facts make the stolen body theory implausible.

The Wrong Tomb Theory

A second theory is that the women went to the wrong tomb. Proponents of this argument state that according to the Gospel accounts, the women visited the grave early in the morning while it was dark. Due to their emotional condition and the darkness, they went to the wrong tomb. Overjoyed to see that it was empty, they rushed back to tell the disciples that Jesus had risen. The disciples in turn ran into Jerusalem to proclaim the resurrection.

The flaw to this explanation is that Christ's opponents knew the exact location of the tomb. The Gospels tell us that Jesus's body was buried in the tomb of Joseph of Arimathea, a member of the Jewish council. If the body remained in the tomb when the apostles began preaching, the authorities could have simply gone to the right tomb, produced the body, and marched it through the streets. This would have put an end to the Christian faith once and for all. Remember, the preaching of the resurrection began in Jerusalem, the city in which Christ was tried and outside of which he was crucified and buried. These factors make this theory very weak.

The Reburial Theory

More recently, some have suggested that Jesus was only temporarily buried in Joseph's tomb until he could be reburied. Allegedly, on Saturday Joseph moved the body to a permanent burial place. The next day the women came to an empty tomb and, not knowing the body had been moved, spread the story of a resurrection.[2]

In response to this implausible scenario, one need only point out the following facts: First and foremost, it does not account for Jesus's twelve bodily appearances to over five hundred people for a forty-day period following this event. Further, it does not account for the testimony of the angels in the record who proclaimed: "He is not here; he has risen" (Matt. 28:6). Also, it provides no plausible explanation for why Joseph of Arimathea, a believer in Christ, would allow the perpetration of the chief priests' false story that Jesus never rose from the dead. Finally, the tomb was sealed by a Roman guard so that no one could take Jesus's body (Matt. 27:62). And it is incredible to suppose that they did not check to see if there was a body there before they began to guard it.

The Hallucination Theory

A fourth theory is that the resurrection of Christ occurred as a hallucination in the minds of the followers of Christ. D. William McNeil articulates this position in his book, *A World History.*

> The Roman authorities in Jerusalem arrested and crucified Jesus. . . . But soon afterwards the dispirited Apostles gathered in an upstairs room and suddenly felt again the heartwarming presence of their master. This seemed absolutely convincing evidence that Jesus's death on the cross had not been the end but the beginning. . . . The Apostles bubbled over with excitement and tried to explain to all who would listen all that had happened.[3]

This position is unrealistic for several reasons. Psychiatrists agree that in order for hallucinations of this type to occur, several conditions must exist. But this situation was not conducive for hallucinations for several reasons:

1. Hallucinations generally occur to people who are imaginative and of a nervous temperament. But Jesus appeared to a variety of people, and not all of them could have been this type of person.
2. Hallucinations are subjective and individual. No two people have the same experience. In this case, over five hundred people (1 Cor. 15:3–8) gave the same account.
3. Hallucinations occur only at particular times and places and are associated with certain events. The resurrection appearances occurred in many different environments and at different times.
4. Hallucinations of this nature occur to those who intensely want to believe. But several (including Thomas and James, the half brother of Jesus) were very skeptical regarding the news of the resurrection.

Those who continue to argue this position still must account for the empty tomb. If the apostles were preaching a fantasized resurrection, the authorities could have produced the body in order to put an end to the apostles' dream. These facts make this theory extremely unlikely.

Jesus Never Died Theory

A fifth theory espouses that Jesus never died on the cross but merely passed out and was mistakenly pronounced dead. After three days he revived, exited the tomb, and appeared to his disciples, who believed he had risen from the dead. This hypothesis was developed in the early nineteenth century, but few hold to it now.

There are several fatal flaws with this theory. First, it is highly unlikely that Jesus could have survived the tortures of the crucifixion. Second, the soldiers who crucified Jesus were experts in executing this type of death penalty and could recognize a dead person from one who was only unconscious. In addition, because the Sabbath was approaching, the Jews asked Pilate to have the three men's legs broken (in order to speed up the process of dying). But when the soldiers came to Jesus, they found that he was already dead. In order to be certain, they thrust a spear into his side, and when blood and water came out separately, it confirmed that he was dead (John 19:31–34). Although the Roman soldiers probably did not understand the scientific explanation, this indicated that the blood cells had begun to separate from the plasma, which only happens when the blood stops circulating.

After being taken down from the cross, Jesus was covered with eighty pounds of spices and embalmed. It is unreasonable to believe that Jesus would revive after three days with no food or water. Even harder to believe is that Jesus could then roll a two-ton stone up an incline, overpower the guards, and then walk several miles to Emmaus. Even if he had done this, he would have appeared to the disciples half dead and desperately in need of medical attention, which would not have prompted their worship of him as God.

In the nineteenth century David F. Strauss, an opponent of Christianity, put an end to any hope in this theory. Although he did not believe in the resurrection, he concluded this theory to be outlandish.

It is impossible that a being who had stolen half-dead out of the sepulcher, who crept about weak and ill, wanting medical treatment, who required bandaging, strengthening, and indulgence, and who still at last yielded to his sufferings, could have given the disciples the impression that he was a conqueror over death and the grave, the Prince of life, an impression that would lay at the bottom of their future ministry.[4]

The Substitution Theory

Another version of the theory that Jesus never died is the substitution theory. Most Muslims, for example, believe Jesus did not die on the cross, nor did he rise from the dead. Indeed, Sura 4:157 declares, "That they said (in boast), 'we have killed Christ Jesus the son of Mary, the Apostle of God'; But they killed him not, nor crucified him. But so it was made to appear to them. . . . For of a surety they killed him not." Some Muslims speculate that Allah transformed a young boy into the likeness of Jesus, and this young boy was crucified in the place of Christ. Other Islamic versions teach that Judas or Simon from Cyrene was crucified in Christ's place. Allah then took Jesus into heaven.

There are several problems with this explanation. Virtually everyone around the cross had a vested interest in the identity of the person being crucified. First, the Jewish and Roman authorities would have taken every precaution to be sure they had detained the right person. Second, the Jewish authorities who sentenced Jesus to death would have made sure that it was he who was being put to death. Third, Jesus was recognized by his mother and the women there who had ministered to him. Fourth, his disciple John, who was at the cross, verified his death (John 19). It is humanly impossible that all these people who knew him so well, including his own mother, were deceived as to who was being crucified before their very eyes. They would have recognized an imposter.

In addition, Jesus's own words disprove this theory. On several occasions he had predicted his death and resurrection. If he did not die on the cross, then the Jewish leaders would have accused him of false prophecy. And finally, if Jesus did not die, he would not have fulfilled his mission. Matthew records that at the Last Supper Jesus said, "This is my blood of the covenant, which is poured out for many for the forgiveness of sins" (Matt. 26:28). John the Baptist identified Jesus as "the Lamb of God, who takes away the sin of the world" (John 1:29). Jesus's mission was to die as the final sacrificial lamb so that forgiveness of sins could be bestowed upon those who believe in his name. If Jesus did not die on the cross, he was preaching a false message; yet even Muslims claim Jesus was a prophet and, as such, would not lie.

The Theory That Jesus's Body Was Eaten by Dogs

John Dominic Crossan, a prominent leader of the Jesus Seminar, introduced another implausible speculation. He argues that the body of Jesus was thrown in a shallow grave and was later dug up and eaten by wild dogs. He writes,

> If the Romans did not observe the Deuteronomic decree, Jesus's dead body would have been left on the cross for wild beasts. And his followers who had fled would know that. If the Romans did observe the decree, the soldiers would have made certain Jesus was dead and then buried him themselves as part of their job. In either case his body left on the cross or in a shallow grave barely covered with dirt and stones, the dogs were waiting. And his followers who had fled, would know that too.[5]

There are several problems with this recent theory. First, it is significant to note that this hypothesis was not proposed until recent times—two thousand years after the fact. Eyewitness opponents of Christianity never suggested this as a possible explanation but instead claimed the disciples stole the body while the guards slept (a theory discussed earlier).

The Gospel writers also went to great lengths to identify the tomb site, even naming the owner—Joseph of Arimathea. Crossan counters this by suggesting that the disciples created a fictitious character:

"The dilemma is painfully clear. Political authority had crucified Jesus and was against him. But, his followers knew, it also took authority or at least authority's permission to bury him. How could one have it both ways? . . . Mark 15:42–46 solves the problem by creating one Joseph of Arimathea."[6]

As indicated earlier, it would have been disastrous for the Gospel writers to make up a character and attribute to him such a high profile position in society. This fact could have easily been researched and discredited by eyewitnesses. In addition, the disciples would have had to invent the account of the guards at the tomb, which would have been easy for their opponents to disprove. Crossan's argument is not consistent with the facts and is not a reasonable option. All the evidence points to a miraculous resurrection of Jesus from the dead.

Finally, given the context, this theory is more fantastic than the resurrection story itself. It overlooks the overwhelming multiple and empirical testimony that the same body that died came to life, was seen and touched, and who spoke, ate food, taught, and performed miracles over a forty-day period. What is more, after these encounters those scared, scattered, and skeptical disciples were transformed overnight into the world's greatest missionary society, and within weeks people from throughout the world heard their testimony, which was preached in the same city where these events had occurred (see Acts 2). It is simpler and easier just to believe in the resurrection.

Jesus Predicts His Resurrection

Another aspect of the resurrection that adds to its supernatural nature is that Jesus actually predicts it on multiple occasions (Matt. 12:38–40; 16:1–4; 17:22–23; 20:18–19; Mark 8:31–32; 9:31; 10:33–34; Luke 9:22; John 2:18–21). The Old Testament also predicts the death and resurrection of the Messiah (Ps. 22:14–18; Isa. 52:13–53:12; Dan. 9:24–27; Zech. 12:10).

After Jesus overturns the Jerusalem temple,

> the Jews demanded of him, "What miraculous sign can you show us to prove your authority to do all this?" Jesus answered, "Destroy this temple, and I will raise it again in three days." The Jews replied, "It has taken forty-six years to build this temple, and you are going to raise it in three days?" But the temple he had spoken of was his body. After he was raised from the dead, his disciples recalled what he had said. Then they believed the Scripture and the words that Jesus had spoken.
>
> John 2:18–22

The sign that Jesus presents to confirm his authority will be his predicted resurrection.

On another occasion, the Jews come to Jesus and demand that he show them a miraculous sign to prove his authority. Jesus is upset by their challenge because he has already performed numerous miracles (see Matthew 8–9). To these hardened individuals, Jesus replies, "Only an evil, adulterous generation would demand a miraculous sign; but the only sign I will give them is the sign of the prophet Jonah. For as Jonah was in the belly of the great fish for three days and three nights, so will the Son of Man be in the heart of the earth for three days and three nights" (Matt. 12:38–40 NLT). The sign to these men will be his prophesied resurrection from the dead. Once again, Jesus predicts his death, burial, and resurrection.

After Peter acknowledges Jesus as the Messiah, "the Son of the living God," his death and resurrection become the focal point of Jesus's message (Matt. 16:16, 21). For example:

> The Son of Man must suffer many things and . . . he must be killed and after three days rise again.
>
> Mark 8:31

> Destroy this temple, and in three days I will raise it up.
>
> John 2:19 NLT

No one can take my life from me. I sacrifice it voluntarily. For I have the authority to lay it down when I want to and also to take it up again. For this is what my Father has commanded.

John 10:18

Now as they came down from the mountain [of transfiguration], Jesus commanded them, saying, "Tell the vision to no one until the Son of Man is risen from the dead."

Matthew 17:9 NKJV

The Son of Man is about to be betrayed into the hands of men, and they will kill Him, and the third day He will be raised up.

Matthew 17:22–23 NKJV

Behold, we are going up to Jerusalem; and the Son of man will be delivered to the chief priests and scribes; and they will condemn him to death, and deliver him to the Gentiles to be mocked and scourged and crucified, and he will be raised on the third day.

Matthew 20:18–19 RSV

These passages reveal that from his early ministry to the end Jesus predicts his death, burial, and resurrection. Making such predictions puts Jesus in a precarious position. If these events do not occur, he could be condemned as a liar and a false prophet, and even his wise sayings would be discredited by a legacy of false prophecy. But his predictions prove to be a powerful apologetic because they are indeed fulfilled, and after his resurrection they echo in the minds of the witnesses who recall his words.

Jesus's Resurrection Is a Fulfillment of Prophecy

Jesus's resurrection proves to be a powerful apologetic for another reason. It is a fulfillment of the Old Testament prophecies about the Messiah (see chap. 7). Isaiah 53:8–10 says,

By oppression and judgment he was taken away.
    And who can speak of his descendants?
For he was cut off from the land of the living;
    for the transgression of my people he was stricken.
He was assigned a grave with the wicked,
    and with the rich in his death,
though he had done no violence,
    nor was any deceit in his mouth.
Yet it was the LORD's will to crush him and cause him to
    suffer,
    and though the LORD makes his life a guilt offering,
he will see his offspring and prolong his days,
    and the will of the LORD will prosper in his hand.

Isaiah's statement that the Messiah will be "cut off from the land of the living" means that the Messiah will be killed. But the Messiah will also "see his offspring and prolong his days," which indicates he will be raised to life. Psalm 16:10 says God's "Holy One" will not remain in Sheol, nor will he "see decay." In addition, Psalm 2 predicts the resurrection:

I will proclaim the decree of the LORD:
He said to me, "You are my Son;
    today I have become your Father.
Ask of me,
    and I will make the nations your inheritance,
    the ends of the earth your possession."

                    Psalm 2:7–8; see also Acts 13:33–35

Not only was the death and resurrection predicted, so were a vast number of surrounding events. The list includes:

1. The Messiah will be pierced (Ps. 22:16; Zech. 12:10).
2. Soldiers will gamble for his clothing (Ps. 22:18).
3. The Messiah will be sold for thirty pieces of silver (Zech. 11:12–13).
4. The Messiah will be killed or "cut off" (Dan. 9:20–27).

5. The Messiah will die a substitutionary death for others (Isa. 53:5–6).
6. The Messiah will stand silent before his accusers (Isa. 53:7).
7. The Messiah will be assigned to the grave with the wicked and the rich (Isa. 53:9).
8. The sacrificial lamb will not have a bone broken (Exod. 12:43–47; Ps. 34:20).
9. The Messiah will be hung on a tree (Deut. 21:22–23).
10. The Messiah will be betrayed by a close friend (Ps. 41:9).

On several occasions, Jesus points out to his disciples that his death and resurrection fulfill Old Testament prophecy (e.g., Matt. 26:31–35, 54; Luke 24:44). In Luke 24 Jesus meets two of his disciples on the road to Emmaus. The men are downcast because their hope for the coming kingdom appears to be crushed with the death of Jesus. Luke records Jesus's words to them: "'How foolish you are, and how slow of heart to believe all that the prophets have spoken! Did not the Christ have to suffer these things and then enter his glory?' And beginning with Moses and all the Prophets, he explained to them what was said in all the Scriptures concerning himself" (Luke 24:25–27). Thus, Jesus presents an apologetic that proves to his disciples that the Old Testament prophets' prediction of his death and resurrection have been fulfilled in his life.

In Luke 24:44–49 Jesus opens the minds of the disciples to understand the Old Testament Scriptures. More than being his greatest miracle, Jesus makes it clear to his disciples that his resurrection is the fulfillment of Old Testament prophecy, which adds to his testimony and becomes foundational for the apologetic the disciples use as they preach to the Jews (Acts 2:22–40; 13:13–43).

Jesus's Death and Resurrection Fulfill the Law

Jesus is the only person who can rightfully be called the Savior of the world, because he is the only one who fulfills the requirements of the Old Testament law and thus is the only one who can atone for the sins of humankind. The writer to the Hebrews states,

> The old system under the law of Moses was only a shadow, a dim preview of the good things to come, not the good things themselves. The sacrifices under that system were repeated again and again, year after year, but they were never able to provide perfect cleansing for those who came to worship.
>
> Hebrews 10:1 NLT

The sacrificial lamb was a foreshadowing of the perfect Lamb, who would fulfill the requirements of the law and pay the price for sin. Under the old system, the sacrifice of lambs could not permanently cleanse a person from sin. It pointed to the coming Messiah, who would take away the sins of the world. According to the Old Testament law, the sacrificial lamb was to be one without blemish (Lev. 23:12, 18). Jesus lived a sinless life, without blemish, and he became the perfect sacrifice for sin (John 1:29; see also John 8:46). There is no individual in any religious system who can atone for our shortfall before our Creator except for Jesus Christ. In him we have one who paid the full price of sin through his death and demonstrated God's acceptance through the resurrection.

Conclusion

In John 11:25 Jesus states, "I am the resurrection and the life. He who believes in me will live, even though he dies; and whoever lives and believes in me will never die." Jesus claims to be the source of life and the victor over physical death. Many "saviors" may make this claim, but in the unique event of his resurrection, Jesus alone confirms his claim. The founders of all religions have died, but Christ alone predicted his death, burial, and resurrection and accomplished this feat.

Jesus uses evidence to support his claims to be the Son of God, and his most powerful evidence is miracles. Miracles confirm God's message and his Messenger (Heb. 2:2–4), and the most important miracle is his resurrection from the dead. Given a theistic context wherein miracles are possible, this remains the best apologetic for the truth of Christianity. Unlike Jesus, however, we have an added burden—namely, to show the historicity of these events. But since there is overwhelming evidence for them, the defense of and appeal to Jesus's miracles remain to date the most effective evidence for the deity of Christ.

4

Jesus's
Apologetic Use of
Reason

As monotheists, the Jews of Jesus's time believed that a reasonable, rational, and morally perfect God created the universe (Matt. 22:37–38). As the Creator (Gen. 1:1, 27), God endowed humans with the capacity for reason and rationality. Reason is part of the "image of God" in which God made people (Col. 3:10), and even in our fallen state, we still retain his image (Gen. 9:6; James 3:9). To be sure, sin has effaced the image of God, but it has not erased it. Unsaved people can still think rationally. Indeed, it was the non-Christian Greek philosopher Aristotle who was the first one known to have set forth the very principles by which all rational beings think—the laws of logic.[1] And despite the well-known difference between the Greek and Hebrew views of the world,[2] there is no essential difference between their use of the basic laws of thought.[3]

Jesus, as Creator and Logos (John 1:1–3; Col. 1:16), also endowed humans with language, by which reasonable ideas can be communicated. As beings made in the image of God, we are designed to know and to live according to truth, and we have the ability to identify error. In Isaiah 1:18, God invites Israel, "Come now, let us reason together."

God wanted the men and women of Israel to use their ability to reason and consider the consequences of their behavior.

A major component of Jesus's mission was to teach and defend truth and to correct error (John 8:32). Through this process, Jesus showed himself to be a brilliant philosopher who used the laws of logic to reveal truth, demolish arguments, and point out error. When we analyze the arguments of Jesus, we soon realize that he was the greatest thinker who ever set foot upon the earth. Contemporary philosopher Dallas Willard states,

> We need to understand that Jesus is a thinker, that this is not a dirty word but an essential work, and that his other attributes do not preclude thought, but only insure that he is certainly the greatest thinker of the human race: "the most intelligent person who ever lived on earth." He constantly uses the power of logical insight to enable people to come to the truth about themselves and about God from the inside of their own heart and mind. Quite certainly it also played a role in his own growth in "wisdom."[4]

Jesus used logic to expose the errors of the Pharisees and teachers of the law. Although he did not articulate the laws of logic or the first principles, he certainly understood them and applied them when he debated the Jewish authorities. *First principles* of knowledge are self-evident (obvious) truths, and they form the foundation of all knowledge. Since a first principle is that from which everything else in its order follows, first principles of knowledge are those basic premises from which all else follows in the realm of knowing.[5]

The Basic Laws of Thought

Aristotle identified the basic forms of rational inference and the basic laws of thought, which are fundamental to all rational thought. Without them, no one can engage in any kind of reasoning process.

The Law of Identity: A is A.

The Law of Noncontradiction: A is not non-A.

The Law of Excluded Middle: Either A or non-A.

In addition to these three laws of thought, Aristotle spelled out various forms of drawing logical deductions from premises. These are called *syllogisms*, of which there are three basic kinds.

Deductive Syllogisms
1. All men and women are sinners.
2. John is a man.
3. Therefore, John is a sinner.

Hypothetical Syllogisms
1. If God exists, then miracles are possible.
2. God exists.
3. Therefore, miracles are possible.

Disjunctive Syllogisms
1. Either John is saved or he is unsaved.
2. John is not unsaved.
3. Therefore, John is saved.

Of course, there are many other valid forms of reasoning, including abbreviated syllogisms (*enthymemes*), in which one or more premises are implied but not stated; a chain of reasoning, in which one premise builds on another (*sorities*); *reductio ad absurdum*; and *a fortiori arguments* (Latin for "with greater force").

Reductio Ad Absurdum
1. Affirming X leads to a logical absurdity.
2. And whatever is logically absurd is false.
3. John holds X.
4. Therefore, X is false.

A Fortiori Arguments
1. A is accepted as true.
2. But the evidence for B is even greater than the evidence for A.

3. Therefore, B should be accepted as true with even greater force than A.

There is also a negative logical movement known as "avoiding the horns of a dilemma." A disjunctive syllogism argues:

1. It is not either this or that.
2. It is not that.
3. Therefore, it is this.

To avoid this conclusion, one must show that the two poles are not logically opposite, and thus there is a third alternative. This rational move takes the following form:

1. It is not either this or that.
2. It is another.
3. Therefore, it does not follow that it is either this or that.

For example one could reason that:

1. Either Paul is rich or poor.
2. He is not poor.
3. Therefore, he is rich.

But this conclusion does not follow, because there is another state between poor and rich. Hence, the conclusion does not follow. Jesus used this maneuver to avoid the apparent dilemmas his opponents proposed to him (see below).

Jesus's Use of Logical Principles and Reasoning

Jesus employed most of the basic forms of reasoning in his discourses. As the Logos (Reason) of God, it is not surprising that he exemplifies these principles of reasoning in his presentation and defense of the truth. Indeed, since logic is based in the very nature of God as the ultimately rational being from whom all rationality flows, it is appropriate to say: "In the beginning was Logic, and Logic was with God, and Logic was of the very nature of God."

Jesus's Uses of the Principle of Noncontradiction

From a human standpoint, the *principle of noncontradiction* is perhaps the most fundamental of all laws of thought since the other laws can be reduced to it.[6] This principle states that it is impossible that contradictory statements be simultaneously true in the same sense. If one statement is true, its contradiction is necessarily false.

As a rational being, Jesus used all the laws of thought; they are unavoidable. But some specific examples of where the law of noncontradiction surfaces in Jesus's discourse will help illustrate the point.

Jesus implies the law of noncontradiction when he warns about false prophets in contrast to true prophets (Matt. 7:15; 24:24). Likewise, he contrasts the children of light with the children of darkness (John 8:12). He repeatedly rebukes those who reject the truth and are in error (John 8:32). Jesus also points out that those who are the children of the devil cannot be the children of God (John 8:42–47). His disciple John later puts the contrast clearly when he says, "Beloved, do not believe every spirit, but test the spirits, whether they are of God; because many false prophets have gone out into the world . . . by this we know the spirit of truth and the spirit of error" (1 John 4:1, 6 NKJV).

Jesus's Use of the Principle of Identity

Like other human beings, Jesus knew intuitively that A is A. Every rational thought and expression he made implied this law. He stated the principle of identity clearly when he said, "But let your 'Yes' be 'Yes,' and your 'No' 'No'" (Matt. 5:37). He knew that without this principle we could not even think or talk coherently. For were the principle of identity not true, then *God* could mean *not God*; *believe* could mean *not believe*, and *good* could mean *not good*.

Jesus's Use of the Principle of the Excluded Middle

This principle states that a proposition must be either true or false. This is a precondition of every thought Jesus expressed, since no affirmation (or negation) can be true and false simultaneously in the same sense.[7] He demonstrated it succinctly when he said, "Whoever is not with me is against me" (Matt. 12:30 ESV), and "He who is not with me is against me" (Luke 11:23). There is no neutrality when it comes to God. Either we believe in him or we do not. Either we accept his lordship or we do not. And those who do not accept it by consequence reject it. Likewise, either we are children of God or we are not (1 John 3:10). We are either walking in the light or walking in the darkness. Indeed, "God is light, and in him there is no darkness at all" (1 John 1:5).

How Jesus Used the Principles of Reasoning

Jesus used many of the standard *Aristotelian* forms of reasoning, though often in enthymeme (abbreviated) form with implied premises. Several familiar stories will illustrate Jesus's use of various forms of reasoning.

Jesus's Use of A Fortiori Arguments

In dialoguing with his opponents, Jesus often used an a fortiori argument. This is a particularly powerful line of reasoning since the opponent already accepts a similar conclusion with even less evidence.

Matthew 12:9–14. Jesus enters a synagogue where there is a man with a shriveled hand. The Jews are looking for a reason to accuse Jesus of working on the Sabbath and thus breaking the fourth commandment, so they confront him: "Is it lawful to heal on the Sabbath?" Jesus replies, "If any of you has a sheep and it falls into a pit on the Sabbath, will you not take hold of it and lift it out? How much more valuable is a man than a sheep! Therefore it is lawful to do good on the Sabbath" (vv. 10–12).

Jesus exposes the fallacy in his critics' logic using an a fortiori argument. He points out that they would be willing to work in order to rescue a distressed sheep on the Sabbath. If that is true, then how much more should they be willing to restore a man who is created in the image of God?

John 7:21–24. Jesus defends his healing on the Sabbath with an a fortiori argument. He points out that in the Old Testament law, circumcision was allowed on the Sabbath. If circumcision can be performed on the Sabbath in obedience to the Mosaic law, why then is it wrong for Jesus to heal a person and make him whole on the Sabbath?

John 10:24–41. Here Jesus is accused of blasphemy because he has declared himself to be God's Son. Jesus points to the testimony of his miracles and asks his opponents, "I have shown you many great miracles from the Father. For which of these do you stone me?" The Jews are infuriated by this claim and state, "We are not stoning you for any of these, . . . but for blasphemy, because you, a mere man, claim to be God" (vv. 31–33).

Jesus answers that Israel's appointed judges were called "gods" not because they were divine beings but because they were God's spokesmen speaking representatively for God (Psalm 82). Now if these men could be called gods because of the authority delegated to them, how much more could Jesus be called the Son of God after all the great miracles he has performed, thus demonstrating God's authority is upon him?

Matthew 7:11. Jesus also says, "If you then, being evil, know how to give good gifts to your children, how much more will your Father who is in heaven give good things to those who ask Him" (NKJV). This is an a fortiori argument in hypothetical form:

1. If evil men and women know how to give good gifts to their children, then how much more does God.
2. Evil men and women know how to give good gifts to their children.
3. Therefore, even more so, God knows how to give good gifts to his children.

Jesus's Use of the Disjunctive Syllogism

Jesus says, "Whoever is not with me is against me" (Matt. 12:30 ESV), and "He who is not with me is against me" (Luke 11:23). Or, "You cannot serve God and Mammon" (Matt. 6:24; Luke 16:13 NKJV). The logic goes like this:

1. Either a person is for Christ or against him.
2. Atheists are not for Christ.
3. Therefore, atheists are against Christ.

Since Jesus claims to be God, there is no neutral position. For either he is accepted as God and is obeyed, or he is not accepted as God and is not obeyed. And if one does not obey God, then he is opposed to God.

Jesus's Use of the Hypothetical Syllogism

Jesus uses a hypothetical syllogism to stop the Pharisees. They accept the Messiah as the Son of David but not the Son of God. Jesus retorts:

1. If David by the Holy Spirit called the Messiah his "Lord," then the Messiah must be more than a mere son of David (i.e., human being).
2. David did call the Messiah "Lord" (Ps. 110:1).
3. Therefore, the Messiah is more than a mere son of David; he is also David's Lord (i.e., God).

Indeed, Jesus devises here an ingenious way to show that as the Messiah he is both God and man. He is man because he is the son of a woman. He is God because David, inspired by the Holy Spirit, says the Messiah is David's "Lord." So, he is both God and man.

Another example of a hypothetical syllogism is in Matthew 6:14: "If you forgive men their trespasses, your heavenly Father will also forgive you" (NKJV). It can be summarized thus:

1. If we forgive others, then God will forgive us.
2. We forgive others.
3. Therefore, God forgives us.

"Judge not, that you be not judged" (Matt. 7:1 NKJV) and many of Jesus's other statements can be put in the form of a hypothetical syllogism from which a logical conclusion follows.

Jesus's Use of the Categorical Syllogism

Luke 6:6–11. Jesus heals a man on the Sabbath. In order to defend himself against the attacks of the legalistic Jews, he uses a categorical syllogism. Before he heals the man with a withered hand, he asks the Pharisees, "Is it lawful on the Sabbath to do good?" (v. 9). They know it is. So his argument takes this form:

1. It is lawful to do good on the Sabbath.
2. Healing someone's hand is good.
3. Therefore, it is lawful to heal a person's hand on the Sabbath.

Matthew 4:4. Jesus often uses categorical syllogisms in abbreviated form. His statement that "one does not live by bread alone" (NRSV) can be used to formulate an argument for the existence of God from need.

1. Human beings need God (i.e., they can't live by bread alone).
2. Whatever we really need, really exists.
3. Therefore, God really exists.

Even the second premise is supported elsewhere by Jesus when he affirms that one's real needs will be met (Matt. 6:25–34; 7:7–11). Common sense dictates that if one needs water, then there must really be water somewhere (whether or not the person finds it). And if one really needs food, then there really is food somewhere (whether or not some die of starvation). Hence, if one really needs God, then there must really be a God somewhere who can fill that need. There is good evidence to believe that men and women really need God. Most people who believe in God acknowledge this, and even great atheists have admitted this implicitly.[8]

Jesus Avoids the Horns of a Dilemma

Jesus is a master at avoiding the horns of a dilemma. This is a very important move for him because otherwise the opponent will refute what he is teaching.

Matthew 22:15–22. Jesus is questioned: "Is it lawful to pay taxes to Caesar, or not?" (v. 17 NKJV). If he says *yes*, then he is recognizing the higher authority of Caesar. If he says *no*, then he is putting himself in opposition to Caesar. But Jesus wishes to do neither; hence the dilemma. His response is brilliant: "Render to Caesar the things that are Caesar's, and to God the things that are God's" (v. 21 ESV). The Pharisees thought they had Jesus trapped in the horns of a dilemma, but he masterfully escapes their trap.

Matthew 22:23–33. The Sadducees, who do not believe in the resurrection, ask Jesus if a woman has outlived seven husbands and bore no children, to which one would she be married in heaven. (Mosaic law required that if a man died childless, his brother must marry the widow and produce an heir in his brother's place; see Deut. 25:5.) Their question is an attempt to show the absurdity of belief in a resurrection. Their trap is clever: Jesus cannot contradict the law of Moses, nor can he deny the resurrection of the dead—a doctrine he has been teaching throughout his ministry. He appears to be faced with only two choices, both of which will lead to an undesired outcome. The Sadducees assume Jesus will have to either deny the law of Moses or reject the idea of the resurrection. The woman cannot be married to all seven brothers at the resurrection, nor is there any reason she should be married to one, since none of the husbands produced an heir.

When we are faced with two unacceptable choices—which is called "going through the horns of the dilemma"—we should look for a third option. Jesus provides a brilliant example when he escapes the horns of a dilemma first by showing that the scenario proposed by the Sadducees is false. In the eternal state the institution of marriage, as well as other earthly institutions, will not be maintained. Second, Jesus indicates that at the resurrection men and women will be like the angels, who do not marry. Jesus knows that the Sadducees regard the Pentateuch as the only authoritative part of the Hebrew Scriptures, so he quotes from their revered text, revealing the error in the Sadducees' understanding of their own Scriptures. God told Moses, "I am the God of your father—the God of Abraham, the God of Isaac, and the God of Jacob" (Exod. 3:6 NKJV). The present tense verb "I am" indicates that God is *presently* their God because they are still alive—that is, the patriarchs have not gone out of existence. Indeed, Moses and Elijah appear alive and conscious on the Mount of Transfiguration (see Matt. 17:1–13; Mark 9:2–13).

Jesus's Use of Reductio Ad Absurdum

Reductio ad absurdum (reduction to absurdity) is an argument that demonstrates that if something is supposed to be true but it leads to a contradiction or absurdity, then it cannot be true. It works this way: The argument begins with the premises your opponent holds. Then you reveal how this leads to a contradiction, and thus your opponent's view is reduced to absurdity.[9] This is a powerful way to reveal the false nature of a view, for if we can show that it leads to a contradiction, then it cannot be true.

Matthew 12:22–28. Jesus uses the reductio ad absurdum argument to respond to the Pharisees' accusation that he is exorcising demons by the power of Satan. Jesus demonstrates that their premise leads to a contradiction: "Every kingdom divided against itself will be ruined, and every city or household divided against itself will not stand. If Satan drives out Satan, he is divided against himself. How then can his kingdom stand? And if I drive out demons by Beelzebub, by whom do your people drive them out?" (vv. 25–27).

Jesus begins with the Pharisees' premise that he drives out demons by the power of Satan. He points out that if he is empowered by Satan to drive out demons, Satan is casting out his own servants. This would mean Satan is divided against himself, and any kingdom, city, or household that develops internal strife will destroy itself. Jesus goes on to point out that there are contemporary Jewish exorcists who also cast out demons. If they believe these men cast out demons by the power of God, why do they not believe that Jesus does so by the power of God? Jesus also has the testimony of miracles that further confirm his authority is from God. Thus, Jesus uses the reductio ad absurdum argument to show that the claim that his authority to cast out demons is from Satan creates a contradictory and absurd conclusion.

Conclusion

The use of reason and logic were essential to the apologetics of Jesus. Using carefully reasoned arguments, he dismantled the arguments of his opponents and pointed out their errors in thinking. Exposing contradictions and fallacies in logic were the methods he employed. Since reason and logical arguments were a part of Jesus's defense, the apologist and all Christians today should make this an area of study as they engage in the battle of ideas.

The mission of transforming lives and bringing people to faith in Christ does not come by moving people emotionally; God does not bypass the mind to speak to the heart. Logic and well-reasoned arguments are required to refute false beliefs and turn people in the direction of truth. Of course, we should not exclude the work of the Holy Spirit and rely exclusively on logic. The work of the Holy Spirit works with a person's reasoning and rational capacity. Dr. James Sire states, it "comes to the 'minds' of God's people—not to some non-rational faculty like our 'emotions' or our 'feelings.' To know God's revelation means to use our minds. This makes knowledge something we can share with others, something we can talk about. God's Word is in words with ordinary rational content."[10] When men and women allow him to, the Holy Spirit reveals truth to their minds before they respond with their emotions and will.

Related to this, theologian Roy B. Zuck reminds us that the Spirit is "the Spirit of truth" (John 14:17; 15:26; 16:13).

He would not teach concepts that failed to meet the tests of truth. (In a correspondence theory of truth, truth is what corresponds to the actual state of affairs.) The Holy Spirit does not guide into interpretations that contradict each other or fail to have logical, internal consistency. . . . The Spirit seeks to aid the Spirit-filled learner to think clearly and accurately. The interpreter must employ principles of reasoning in making inductions, deductions, analogies, and comparisons.[11]

Truth corresponds to reality and is internally consistent. Therefore, logic and reason must be used to interpret and discern truth from error. Jesus demonstrated this as he used reason to expose error and present truth. So the use of the basic principles and procedures of reasoning were an essential part of Jesus's apologetic. All people, even in their fallen state, have this ability, and Jesus used it in attempting to help them see the truth.

5

Jesus's
Apologetic Use of
Parables

It is a well-known fact that Jesus was the greatest storyteller who ever lived. His parables captivated audiences, taught valuable lessons, and were memorable. When we call someone a "good Samaritan" or a "prodigal son," many all over the world know what we mean because of the unforgettable parables told by Jesus. One of the best ways to communicate truth is to illustrate it through stories, which are also an effective way to penetrate hardened hearts that are not receptive to a direct presentation of the truth.

Jesus told parables to teach valuable spiritual lessons. His stories illustrated truth, pointed out error, transformed thinking, and called for a response from the audience. There were minimal characters in the stories, and the audience was able to recognize the identity of the characters to which Jesus referred. Usually he identified the characters as: (1) God or himself, (2) the audience, and (3) the Jewish leaders. As the drama unfolded, Jesus illustrated a truth, exposed the false ideas, and called for a proper response.

Apologetics in the Parables

Jesus's parables also had an apologetic character. Through the use of these creative stories, Jesus made a declaration and defense of his claim to be the divine Son of God. The images he selected were used as references to God in both the Old Testament and the later Jewish literature. He used subtle but powerful logic in many of his parables, often in support of his deity. The logic can be summarized as follows:

1. In the Old Testament, God refers to himself as X.
2. I am X.
3. Therefore, I am God.

Dr. Philip Payne wrote his doctoral dissertation at Cambridge University on this topic. He states, "Out of the fifty-two recorded narrative parables, twenty depict Him in imagery which in the Old Testament typically referred to God. The frequency with which this occurs indicates that Jesus regularly depicted Himself in images which were particularly appropriate for depicting God."[1] Applying these images to himself indicated Jesus's self-understanding as the divine Son of God and communicated this truth to his audience. In the parables he revealed his divinity, defended his claim, and validated his ministry. Entrance into the kingdom of God and one's eternal destiny depend on how a person responds to Jesus's words. The authority to judge and grant eternal life is reserved for God, and this is the authority Jesus claims for himself.

Jesus's Implicit Claim to Deity in the Parables

Philip Payne identifies ten prominent images used in the parables as a reference to God in the Old Testament that Jesus applies to himself.[2] His repeated use of such images indicates that he wants his audience to recognize his divinity and that he is carrying out the will of God in his ministry on earth.

The Imagery of God as the Sower

The sower is a prominent image in Jesus's parables, reflecting several passages in the Old Testament in which God is pictured as a sower or planter (e.g., Num. 24:6–7; Pss. 80:8–16; 104:13–16; Jer. 2:21; 11:17; 12:2; 17:8). God is depicted as a sower who plants a vine—which symbolizes the nation of Israel in a garden valley—and cares for the vine so that it will produce fruit. In the writings of the prophets, the vine does not produce fruit and is trampled and abandoned—representing God's judgment on the nation of Israel.

In several parables Jesus applies the image of the sower to himself. For instance, in Luke 8:5–8 he pictures himself as the sower who scatters the seed, which is the Word of God. The different types of soil indicate the various ways in which God's Word is received. Jesus uses this parable to show that he reflects the image of God and to declare that as the Son of God, the destiny of men and women rests upon their response to his words.

God Is the Director of the Harvest

A second image used in the parables is that of the director of the harvest. God not only plants the seed but he also gathers the crops at harvesttime, which in the Old Testament represents the day of the Lord (e.g., Isa. 27:3–12; Jer. 51:33; Hos. 2:21–23; 6:11; Joel 3:13). In these passages God waits patiently for Israel or for foreign nations to repent of sin, but in the end God's judgment (pictured as a harvest) comes upon them.

In Matthew 13:24–30 and Mark 4:26–29, Jesus is portrayed as the director of the harvest. He has sown his seeds and awaits the day of harvest. At harvesttime, which is judgment day, he sends his servants to harvest, and men and women from all the nations receive his judgment. Jesus declares that as the divine Son of God, he has the authority of God to carry out his judgment on the souls of men and women. In John 5:26–27 he states, "For as the Father has life in himself, so he has granted the Son also to have life in himself. And he has given him authority to execute judgment, because he is the

Son of Man" (ESV). Through this parable Jesus reinforces his claims that he possesses authority from the Father and that he will be the judge at the end of the age.

God Is the Rock

A third image is that of a rock, which is used to describe God, especially in the Psalms (Pss. 19:14; 28:1; 42:9; 61:2; 62:2; 71:3; 78:35). The rock in many of these passages symbolizes a sure and unshakable foundation upon which a believer can trust. Jesus uses the parable of the wise and foolish builders to state that those who build their lives upon his teachings have built upon a sure foundation (Matt. 7:24–26; Luke 6:46–49). This affirms that his words are the words of God, that obeying his teachings is equivalent to obeying God, and since God is an unshakable foundation, so is Jesus.

God Is the Shepherd

A shepherd is the fourth image Jesus uses in the parables. In the Old Testament God is portrayed as a shepherd who cares for his people as a shepherd cares for his sheep. In Ezekiel 34:1–22 God declares that he is a shepherd who seeks his lost sheep and that those who have not properly cared for his sheep will be held accountable. David declares in the twenty-third psalm that "The LORD is my shepherd." When Jesus portrays himself as the good shepherd (see John 10:1–18), we can conclude that he is drawing from passages such as Ezekiel 34 and Psalm 23—identifying himself as the good shepherd and therefore implicitly claiming to be God.

God Is the Bridegroom

A fifth image used in Jesus's parables is the bridegroom. In the Old Testament God is pictured as a bridegroom and the people of Israel as his bride (Isa. 49:18; 54:5–8; 62:4; Jer. 2:2; 3:1–14; Ezek. 16:8–14; Hos. 2:1–13). When he is asked why his disciples do not fast as John's disciples and the Pharisees do, Jesus responds that the guests of the wedding do not fast when the bridegroom is among them (Matt. 9:14–15; Mark 2:18–20; Luke 5:33–35)—applying the bridegroom image to himself.

God Is the Father

A sixth image is that of a father. Throughout the Old Testament, Yahweh is called Father (Deut. 32:6; 2 Sam. 7:14; Pss. 68:5; 89:26; 103:13; Jer. 31:9; Mal. 1:6; 2:10). In the parable of the prodigal son (Luke 15:11–32), Jesus defends his association with sinners by identifying his actions as analogous to God the Father, who joyfully welcomes repentant sinners into his family.

God Is the Forgiver of Sins

A seventh image is the provider of forgiveness. In the Old Testament, Yahweh alone can grant forgiveness of sins (Exod. 32:32; 34:7; Lev. 4:20, 26, 31; 5:10; 6:7; Num. 14:18–20; Deut. 21:8; Pss. 25:18; 32:1–5; Isa. 33:24). Jesus is criticized for allowing a sinful woman to anoint his feet, but he defends himself by telling the story of two debtors. He explains through this parable that the woman knows she is a sinner, and so her love will be great when he forgives her, because she recognizes the vastness of her debt (Luke 7:41–43; see vv. 36–50). When he claims the authority to forgive sins, the Jewish scribes attack him: "Who can forgive sins but God alone?" (Mark 2:7). The scribes do not realize that their accusation actually confirms that Jesus is God, the forgiver of sins.

God Is the Vineyard Owner

An eighth image is that of the vineyard owner, which appears in several Old Testament passages (e.g., Deut. 8:8; Ps. 80:8–16; Isa. 5:1–7; 27:2–6; 65:21; Jer. 2:21; Ezek. 28:26; Hos. 2:15; 10:1; Joel 1:7). In Matthew 20:1–16 Jesus defends his acceptance of sinners by telling the story of a generous vineyard owner. The Pharisees feel they should have greater recognition because they have been serving God for a great length of time compared to sinners who came to repentance later in life. Jesus identifies himself as the generous vineyard owner who rewards all people despite the length of time they have been in his service. He uses this parable to support his claim to have the authority to give blessings to anyone who receives his invitation to the kingdom—an authority that is reserved for God.

The Use of the Word LORD (Yahweh)

A ninth image is related to the word LORD. In the Old Testament, this word is used only as the name of Yahweh (God); it is never used for any other being. But Jesus applies it to himself in his parables.

In his ministry, Jesus accepts those who address him as LORD (John 20:28). In parables such as the doorkeeper (Mark 13:32–37), the ten virgins (Matt. 25:1–13), and the talents (Luke 19:12–27), Jesus applies the title of LORD to himself. These stories characterize him as having the authority to grant entrance (and reward) into the kingdom and to judge those who will not enter.

God Is King

A tenth image is that of a king, and it is used of Yahweh many times in the Old Testament (e.g., 1 Sam. 12:12; Pss. 10:16; 11:4; 22:28; 24:7–10; 29:10; 44:4; 47:2–9; 48:2). In Luke 19:11–27 Jesus tells the story of a nobleman who leaves to receive his coronation as king. During his absence he distributes minas (about three months wages) among his three servants. Jesus identifies himself in this parable as the king who executes judgment upon his return. The authority to judge is reserved for God alone, and Jesus claims that authority.

Other Claims to Deity in the Parables

In several parables Jesus presents an apologetic argument for his claim to deity and as a defense of his ministry. He often does this with great subtlety and creativity, and it has a powerful apologetic appeal.

The Parable of the Prodigal Son

One of the most famous parables is that of the prodigal son (Luke 15:11–32). The reason Jesus tells this story is explained in 15:1–2. He associates with the tax gatherers and sinners, intentionally reaching out to them in friendship and teaching them spiritual truths. "But the Pharisees and the teachers of the law muttered, 'This man welcomes sinners and eats with them'" (v. 2).

The Pharisees and scribes question Jesus's conduct. If this is the Son of God, why does he associate with the lowest members of society? The teachers of the law judge this segment of society because they believe these people have sold themselves to the Roman government and prostitutes. This sin makes them spiritually dead and separated from Israel's religious community.[3] The Pharisees and scribes believe that if Jesus was the Messiah, he would know that these people reject Jewish law and do not deserve entrance into the kingdom of God. The ones who deserve the attention of the Messiah are those who have been faithful to the law, not the sinners who have chosen to live a life of rebellion.

In this context Jesus tells the story of the prodigal son to illustrate truth, expose the false ideas of the Pharisees, and call for a proper response. He also presents an apologetic defense of his ministry and conduct in this story. The two sons in the story represent those who comprise his audience.

In this parable the younger son demands his inheritance, rejects his father's teaching, and journeys to a foreign land, where he lives a life of frivolity and loses all he has. He then repents and returns home, ashamed and humiliated. While he is still far away, the father runs to greet his son and celebrates his return. The elder brother is upset at the celebration for his brash younger brother and refuses to join the party despite the pleading of his father.

Jesus tells the story in such a way that we know who the characters represent: The father in this story is God the Father. The younger of the two sons is the sinners and tax gatherers who listen to Jesus's teaching. The elder son is the Pharisees and scribes.

Jesus illustrates several points in this parable: First, God's love extends to all people who receive his Son and repent of their sins—including sinners and tax gatherers. God longs for them to return to him and enter into his kingdom. Second, the elder son represents the Pharisees who have hardened their hearts and will not accept God's revelation revealed in his Son, Jesus. Also, they have failed to reflect the character of God in their response. They have hardened their hearts to their fellow men and women, whom they were given charge to teach and to seek their spiritual welfare. God pursues sinners because of his great love for all people, and he rejoices when they repent. If the Pharisees had the heart of God, they too would rejoice at the repentance of sinners.

The apologetic argument Jesus presents is that he is the Son of God and that his ministry and conduct reflect the heart of the Father, who seeks the lost. Jesus's ministry represents the mission that is at the center of his Father's heart, and he has exposed the Pharisees' hardened hearts, unbelief, and rejection of God's mission. True faith is displayed in love for sinners, while false faith is revealed in spiritual pride.

The Parable of the Vineyard Owner

Another example is the story of the owner of the vineyard (Matt. 21:33–46). The Jews would have recognized this analogy because it was used in Isaiah 5. In this passage God is the owner of the vineyard, which is Jerusalem, the capital of the nation of Israel. Isaiah warns the children of Israel that the owner of the vineyard will come to judge the nation for their sin and they will go into exile.

The Jews very likely recognize Jesus's reference to this passage and quickly remember the story's theme. The wicked tenants who are placed in charge of the vineyard are the chief priests and Pharisees (Matt. 21:45). The servants who are mistreated by the tenants when they are sent to collect rent represent the prophets of the Old and New Testaments, who were persecuted for presenting the message from God. The son of the vineyard owner symbolizes Jesus Christ, the Son of God.

The full nature of the wicked tenants is revealed when they murder the son of the vineyard owner. In refusing to accept the message of John the Baptist and now Jesus, the Jewish leaders are rejecting God's final messenger. Jesus then teaches that after numerous acts of kindness and mercy, the patience of the owner will come to an end and judgment will fall upon the wicked tenants. This adds a prophetic element to the parable; Jesus predicts his death and the future judgment upon the nation of Israel.

Jesus builds on the rejection motif, but the story does not end with the rejection of the son. He then quotes Psalm 118:22–25, shifting the imagery from the son of the vineyard owner to builders who reject the chief cornerstone. In this analogy the stone that was rejected becomes the most important stone of the building—the capstone. Jesus then states that this stone will destroy those who oppose him. By killing the son, the tenants destroy themselves, and the builders who reject the cornerstone bring ruin upon themselves. Jesus predicts his rejection in the parable of the vineyard but also predicts his exaltation in the analogy of the cornerstone.[4]

The first lesson we learn from this parable is the patience and long-suffering of God, who sent prophet after prophet entreating Israel to turn and repent. In the same way, rather than enacting swift judgment, God sends his Son in one last attempt to reach his people who have rejected his message. The second lesson is that Jesus exposes the wickedness of Israel in spurning God's love. Third, we learn that God's patience will come to an end, and his judgment will fall on those who reject him. Finally, the special status will be taken away for a time from Israel and given to another group of people who will produce fruit.

The apologetic defense Jesus presents in this parable is: (1) His rejection by the leadership of Israel is a fulfillment of Old Testament prophecy. (2) Jesus's teachings will be shown to be true when his prophecies of the destruction of Jerusalem, his death, and his exaltation come to pass.

Conclusion

Jesus's use of parables demonstrates the value of stories to persuade an audience and convey a message that cannot always be achieved by direct discourse. Perhaps this is part of the reason for Jesus's reluctance to be more forthright in his claim for deity. As a direct claim, it is too much for most people to accept. Indeed, since the Jewish leaders of Jesus's day understand that the Messiah will be God, this may in part explain why Jesus never publicly says, "I am the Messiah." Both direct admissions that he is the Messiah are made in private—first to a Samaritan woman (John 4:25–26) and then to the high priest at his trial (Mark 14:61–62). And his admission in the latter case draws a violent reaction and the charge of blasphemy (Mark 14:64). Indeed, even more covert claims to deity evoke a strong response (Mark 2:5–7; John 10:30–38). Little wonder that Jesus uses parables to lessen the offense of more overt claims.

The indirect method of claiming deity through story has the added value of eliciting self-discovery. Only after Jesus has taught his disciples in parables does he ask them who they think he is. This elicits that great confession of Peter: "You are the Christ [Messiah], the Son of the living God!" (Matt. 16:16). So by adding the interrogative, Socratic method to the parabolic method, Jesus is able to persuade his followers of the most outlandish claim any human being has ever made—that he is God Almighty in human flesh! This was an incredible apologetic technique, the value of which we need to exploit as we do pre-evangelism in this postmodern world that is so opposed to the claims of Christ (see chap. 11).

6

Jesus's Apologetic Use of Discourse

Jesus often used direct discourse to establish his claims to deity. Even here, though, the apologetic was often indirect on the surface but powerful to the Jewish audience he was addressing. We will first examine the Jewish monotheistic context and then consider some of his claims to deity over against this background.

Proclamation versus Parable

As discussed in chapter 5, parables were a softer way to get across a strong message. In addition, they had the advantage of helping to elicit a positive response. The apologetic value to persuade the audience of the truth of Christ being proclaimed was powerful, so it is understandable that Jesus used it so often.

Nonetheless, there is also a role for direct proclamation, and it is instructive to consider when and why Jesus used it. All the parables of Jesus appear in the Synoptic Gospels (Matthew, Mark, and Luke); most of the direct discourse is recorded by John. It is well-known that the Synoptics stress Jesus's public ministry and John emphasizes private ministry. John is also famous for the "I am" statements of Jesus that contain many of his claims to deity. What is not as widely known is the reason that Jesus spoke more directly at some times than others.

Some critics claim it is unlikely that Jesus actually made the direct discourse statements such as the "I am" assertions found in the Gospel of John—particularly those that stress his deity. This allegation of inauthenticity is because the "I am" statements are not found anywhere in the Synoptic Gospels and they are unlike Jesus's parables. In addition to Jesus's claim to be the "I am" (God) who existed before Abraham (John 8:58), John alone contains the seven famous "I am" statements of Christ.

1. "I am the bread of life" (6:35).
2. "I am the light of the world" (8:12).
3. "I am the gate for the sheep" (10:7, 9).
4. "I am the good shepherd" (10:11, 14).
5. "I am the resurrection and the life" (11:25).
6. "I am the way and the truth and the life" (14:6).
7. "I am the true vine" (15:1).

The fact that the "I am" statements are unique to John, however, in no way proves that they are not authentic. The critics' argument overlooks many important factors. One could argue equally that any of the Synoptic sayings that are not duplicated in one of the other books also cannot be trusted.

First, several reasons can be provided for the authenticity of the "I am" statements: (1) No other first-century religious leader is known to have used similar statements. The format is virtually unparalleled. (2) On at least two occasions, the Synoptic Gospels use the "I am" form of address (Mark 6:50; 13:6 NLT). (3) The "I am" statements found in John contain nothing that is not implicit in similar statements in the Synoptics. They paint a picture of a man whose "words would last forever, pronounce the forgiveness of sins, describe humanity's eternal destiny as dependent on its relation to him, demand absolute loyalty from his disciples, offer rest for the weary and salvation for the lost, promise to be with his followers always, and guarantee that God would grant them any prayer requested in his name."[1]

Second, there is no good reason that both John and the Synoptics cannot be taken as independently authentic. Both agree in all major areas of overlap in relating the life of Christ including his being heralded by John, performing miracles, dying on the cross, and rising from the dead. And when there is a direct parallel on Christ's teaching, they agree almost word for word.

Third, other typically Johannine statements are not unique to John. There are clear examples of this type of statement in Matthew 11:25–27 and Luke 10:21–22.

Fourth, the Synoptics are not without "I am" statements of Christ. Jesus says to the high priest, "I am [the Christ]" (Mark 14:62). The same Greek words are also quoted when Jesus says, "Take courage! *I am he.* Don't be afraid" (Mark 6:50 NKJV, emphasis added). Stauffer offers three arguments for translating this phrase "I am he" rather than the usual "It is I." First, it was Passover time when this divine revelatory phrase was fixed in the Jewish ritual at the time. Second, it was during a storm when "the appearance of Jesus walking on the sea can be regarded here as an epiphany of the God who rules the waters."[2] Third, the phrases "take heart" and "have no fear" that precede the "I am" statements were already an established part of the Old Testament self-revelation of Yahweh (e.g., Ps. 46:2; Isa. 43:1). Indeed, the Jewish Qumran Damascus Document states, "Seekest thou the God of Gods? I am He," which is followed in the next chapter by, "I am He, fear not, for I am before the days were."[3] Indeed, the phrase "I am he" (Greek, *ego eimi*) is based in the Old Testament proclamation by God that he is God (e.g., Deut. 5:6; 32:39; Ps. 46:11; Isaiah 40–45). Its use by Jesus in both the Synoptics and John reveals his claim to deity. As Stauffer argues, " 'I am He'—meant: where I am, there God is, there God lives and speaks, class, asks, acts, decides, loves, chooses, forgives, rejects, suffers, and dies. . . . God himself had become man, more human than any other man in the wide expanse of history."[4]

Fifth, there are parallel self-revelatory statements in a contemporary apocalyptic document, the Ethiopian Ascension of Isaiah (AD 68). It reads, "And all the people in the world will believe him. And they will sacrifice to him and they will serve him, saying, 'This is God and beside him there is none other. . . .' And many believers and saints having seen Him for whom they were hoping, who was crucified, Jesus, the Lord Christ, and those also who were believers in Him."[5] Since this work was probably written well before John wrote his Gospel (ca. AD 90), the self-revelatory statements claiming deity are much earlier and independent of John. For this reason, they lend further support to the authenticity of John's statements.

Sixth, the Gospel of John contains both first person statements of Christ and also third person statements that are more common in the Synoptics. A possible reason for this may appear in John 10, where he turns from third person (vv. 1–6) to first person (vv. 7–18) when the audience does not understand what he is saying (see also John 4:26), providing insight as to why Jesus makes this shift: "'I tell you the truth, the man who does not enter the sheep pen by the gate, but climbs in by some other way, is a thief and a robber.' Jesus used this figure of speech, but *they did not understand* what he was telling them. Therefore, Jesus said again, 'I tell you the truth, *I am* the gate for the sheep'" (John 10:1, 6–7, emphasis added). Since John stresses the antagonism of the Jewish leaders to Jesus (see e.g., John 5:16, 18; 7:1; 10:31), it is understandable that his "I am" deity claims occur in this Gospel.

Seventh, the seven *I am*s in the Gospel of John no more prove he fabricated them than the seven *signs* (miracles) he used to support his theme (see John 20:30–31). Both are chosen by John from all the signs and sayings of Jesus to make his point. It just so happens that there is no overlap of sayings in John with those in the Synoptics, but why should there be if he is consciously giving supplementary information from the great wealth of material that "even the world itself could not contain" (John 21:25)?

Even so, there is an overlap with the Synoptics for the signs or miracles John records. For example, Jesus walking on water (Matt. 14:22–32; Luke 9:10–17; John 6:16–21), the feeding of the five thousand (Matt. 14:13–21; Mark 6:30–44; John 6:1–13), and Christ's resurrection (Matt. 28:1–10; Mark 16; Luke 24:1–49; John 20) are in both John's Gospel and the Synoptics. The fact that there is no significant difference from the Synoptics in the way John reports these signs also argues for the authenticity of the sayings he reports. Since there is no reason to doubt John's authenticity when reporting the signs of Jesus, there is no reason to doubt him when he reports the sayings of Jesus.

Eighth, D. A. Carson states, "The precise form [of 'I am' statements] is unique to the Fourth Gospel, but . . . the Synoptics display other forms of 'I' utterances, while Synoptic parables provide much of the subject matter of Johannine 'I-sayings.'"[6]

Finally, it is John who records that Jesus promises divine activation of the memories of the apostles: "The Counselor, the Holy Spirit, whom the Father will send in my name, will teach you all things and will remind you of everything I have said to you" (John 14:26; see also John 16:13). With this claim in mind, it is unlikely John would risk putting words in Jesus's mouth that would show him (John) to be inaccurate. If their memories were supernaturally activated by the Holy Spirit, then there is no real problem as to how the writers of the Gospels could remember decades later what Jesus had said.[7]

The Jewish Monotheistic Context

Not only was there a *cultural context* for Jesus using more direct discourse, as recorded by John, but there is also a *theological context* for understanding Jesus's claims to be God. Whether direct or indirect, these assertions can only fully be appreciated in light of the monotheistic context in which Jesus spoke them. This monotheistic context includes at least three factors: (1) There is one and only one God who created this world and is transcendent over it. (2) Yahweh (translated LORD) is unique in both title and nature.

This term is never used in the Old Testament for anyone except the one and only living and true God. (3) There were certain things that only God (Yahweh) could do, such as create, raise the dead, forgive sins, perform true miracles, share God's glory, accept worship, and judge the dead. For any mortal to claim to do any of these things was sheer blasphemy—an act worthy of death in the Jewish culture. It is against this background that we must see the unique claims of Christ.

The Unity of God

The Scriptures affirm God's absolute unity from the beginning to the very end:

Genesis 1:1—"In the beginning *God* [not *gods*] created the heavens and the earth."

Exodus 20:3—"You shall have *no other gods* before *me*."

Deuteronomy 6:4—"Hear, O Israel: The LORD our God, the LORD is one."

Isaiah 44:6—"I am the first and I am the last; *apart from me there is no God.*"

Isaiah 45:18—"*I* am the LORD, and there is *no other*" (emphasis added).

Jesus, steeped in the teachings of the Old Testament, affirms this same truth:

Mark 12:29—"'The most important one [command],' answered Jesus, 'is this: "Hear, O Israel, the Lord our God, the Lord is one."'"

Likewise, the apostle Paul, a converted rabbi, confirms the same teaching:

1 Corinthians 8:4—"We know that an idol *is* nothing in the world, and that there *is* no other God but one."

Ephesians 4:6—[There is] "one God and Father of all, who is over all and through all and in all."

1 Timothy 2:5—"For there is one God and one mediator between God and men, the man Christ Jesus."

The Uniqueness of God

Not only does the Old Testament teach the unity of God (Yahweh), but it also declares his uniqueness. He announces to Moses and Israel: "I am the LORD your God. . . . You shall have no other gods before me" (Exod. 20:2–3). He alone claims sovereignty over life: "Now see that I, even I, am He, and there is no God besides Me; I kill and I make alive" (Deut. 32:39 NKJV). When he creates life from dust through Moses, even the magicians of Egypt cry out, "This is the finger of God" (Exod. 8:19). Likewise, only Yahweh can forgive sins (Isa. 43:25) and judge the dead (Joel 3:12). Finally, Yahweh declares through Isaiah, "I am the LORD, that is My name; and My glory I will not give to another" (Isa. 42:8 NKJV).

Jesus's Claims to Be the Monotheistic God

It is with this background that Jesus's unique claims to deity recorded in the Gospel of John and elsewhere must be understood, for he asserts that he is Yahweh himself and he does what only Yahweh could do. This is manifest on numerous occasions. The following are some of the more significant ones.

Jesus's Claim to Be Yahweh

Yahweh is the special name given by God for himself in the Old Testament. It is the name revealed to Moses: "God said to Moses, 'I AM WHO I AM'" (Exod. 3:14 NKJV). While other titles for God may be used of humans (*Adonai* [Lord] in Gen. 18:1–2) or false gods (*elohim*, translated "gods" in Deut. 6:14), *Yahweh* is only used to refer to the one true God, and no other person or thing is to be worshiped or served (Exod. 20:5). Isaiah writes, "Thus saith the LORD

[Yahweh]. . . . I am the first, and I am the last; and beside me there is no God" (Isa. 44:6 KJV), and, "I am the LORD [Jehovah]; that is my name; and my glory I will not give to another, neither my praise unto graven images" (Isa. 42:8 KJV).

Yet Jesus claims to be Jehovah on many occasions. He prays, "And now, O Father, glorify thou me with thine own self with the glory which I had with thee before the world was" (John 17:5 KJV). He also declares, "I am the first and the last" (Rev. 1:17)—precisely the words used by Yahweh in Isaiah 42:8. Jesus also says, "I am the good shepherd" (John 10:11), which is significant because the Old Testament says, "The LORD [Yahweh] is my shepherd" (Ps. 23:1). Further, Jesus claims to be the judge of all people (Matt. 25:31–46; John 5:26–30), but Joel quotes the Lord as saying, "for there I will sit to judge all the nations round about" (Joel 3:12 RSV). Likewise, Jesus speaks of himself as the "bridegroom" (Matt. 25:1) while the Old Testament identifies Yahweh in this way (Isa. 61:20; 62:5; Hos. 2:16). While the psalmist declares, "The LORD is my light" (Ps. 27:1), Jesus says, "I am the light of the world" (John 8:12).

Jesus's Claim to Be the Great "I AM"

When God reveals himself to Moses at the burning bush, it is as Yahweh, the one who says his name is "I AM" (Exod. 3:14). Thus, the strongest claim Jesus makes to be Yahweh is in John 8:58, where he says, "Before Abraham was, I AM" (NKJV). This statement claims not only Jesus's existence before Abraham but also his equality with the "I AM" of Exodus 3:14. The Jews around him clearly understand his meaning, and they pick up stones to kill him for blaspheming (John 8:59; see also John 10:31–33). The same basic claim to be the "I AM" is made in Mark 14:62 and John 18:5–6.

Jesus claims equality with God in other ways, including assuming for himself the prerogatives of God. He says to a paralytic, "Son, your sins are forgiven." The scribes correctly respond, "Who can forgive sins but God alone?" (Mark 2:5–7). So to prove that his claim is not an empty boast, Jesus heals the man, offering direct proof that what he has said about forgiving sins is true also.

Another prerogative Jesus claims is the power to raise and judge the dead: "I tell you the truth, a time is coming and has now come when the dead will hear the voice of the Son of God and those who hear will live . . . and come out—those who have done good will rise to live, and those who have done evil will rise to be condemned" (John 5:25, 29). He removes all doubt about his meaning when he adds, "For just as the Father raises the dead and gives them life, even so the Son gives life to whom he is pleased to give it" (John 5:21). But the Old Testament clearly teaches that only God is the giver of life (Deut. 32:39; 1 Sam. 2:6), the one who raises the dead (Ps. 2:7), and the only judge (Deut. 32:35; Joel 3:12). Jesus boldly assumes for himself powers that only God has.

Jesus also claims that he should be honored as God. He says that all men and women should "honor the Son just as they honor the Father. He who does not honor the Son does not honor the Father, who sent him" (John 5:23). The Jews listening know that no one should claim to be equal with God in this way, and the Jews wanted even more to kill him (John 5:18).

Jesus Claims to Be Messiah-God

Even the Qu'ran recognizes that Jesus was called the Messiah (Sura 5:17, 75), but the Old Testament teaches that the coming Messiah will be God himself. So when Jesus says he is that Messiah, he is also claiming to be God. For example, the prophet Isaiah calls the Messiah "Mighty God" (Isa. 9:6). The psalmist writes of the Messiah, "Your throne, O God, will last for ever and ever" (Ps. 45:6: cf. Heb. 1:8). Psalm 110:1 records a conversation between the Father and the Son: "The LORD [Yahweh] says to my Lord [*Adonai*]: 'Sit at my right hand'" (v. 1). Jesus applies this passage to himself in Matthew 22:43–44. In the great messianic prophecy of Daniel 7, the Son of Man is called the "Ancient of Days" (v. 22), a phrase used twice in the same passage in reference to God the Father (vv. 9, 13). Jesus also says he is the Messiah at his trial before the Sanhedrin:

The high priest asked him, "Are you the Christ [using the Greek word for *Messiah*], the Son of the Blessed One?" "I am," said Jesus. "And you will see the Son of Man sitting at the right hand of the Mighty One and coming on the clouds of heaven." The high priest tore his clothes. "Why do we need any more witnesses?" he asked. "You have heard the blasphemy."

Mark 14:61–64

Thus, in saying he is the Messiah, Jesus is claiming to be God (see also Matt. 26:62–65; Luke 22:66–71).

Jesus Claims to Be God by Accepting Worship

The Old Testament records God's words through Moses forbidding worship of anyone other than God (Exod. 20:1–5; Deut. 5:6–9). The New Testament provides examples of Barnabas and Paul refusing to allow the men and women of Lystra to worship them (Acts 14:8–18) and an angel stopping John from worshiping him (Rev. 22:8–9). But Jesus accepts worship on numerous occasions: A healed leper worships him (Matt. 8:2 NKJV), and a ruler kneels before him with a request (Matt. 9:18). After he stills the storm, "those who were in the boat worshiped him, saying, 'Truly you are the Son of God'" (Matt. 14:33). A Canaanite woman (Matt. 15:25), the mother of James and John (Matt. 20:20), and the Gerasene demoniac (Mark 5:6) all kneel in worship before Jesus without one word of rebuke. A blind man says, "'Lord, I believe,' and he worshiped him" (John 9:38). But Christ also elicits worship in some cases, as when Thomas sees the risen Christ and cries out, "My Lord and my God!" (John 20:28). This could only be done by a person who seriously considers himself to be God.

Jesus Claims to Have Equal Authority with God

Jesus also puts his words on a par with God's. "You have heard that it was said to the people long ago. . . . But I tell you . . ." (Matt. 5:21–22) is repeated over and over again. "All authority in heaven and on earth has been given to me. Therefore go and make disciples

of all nations" (Matt. 28:18–19). God had given the Ten Commandments to Moses, but Jesus says, "A new commandment I give you:
Love one another" (John 13:34). Jesus also says, "Until heaven and
earth disappear, not the smallest letter, not the least stroke of a pen,
will by any means disappear from the Law" (Matt. 5:18), but later
he says of his own words, "Heaven and earth will pass away, but my
words will never pass away" (Matt. 24:35). Speaking of those who
reject him, Jesus says, "That very word which I spoke will condemn
him at the last day" (John 12:48). There is no question that Jesus
expects his words to have equal authority with God's declarations
in the Old Testament.

Jesus Claims to Be God by Requesting Prayer in His Name

Jesus not only asks us to believe in him and obey his commandments, but he also instructs us to pray in his name: "And I will do
whatever you ask in my name. . . . You may ask me for anything in
my name, and I will do it" (John 14:13–14). "If you remain in me and
my words remain in you, ask whatever you wish, and it will be given
you" (John 15:7). Jesus even insists, "No one comes to the Father
except through me" (John 14:6). In response to this the disciples
not only pray *in* Jesus's name (1 Cor. 5:4) but they pray *to* him (Acts
7:59). Jesus certainly intends that his name be invoked both *before*
God and *as* God in prayer.

Jesus Claims to Be the Son of Man

Some causal readers assume that the phrase "Son of Man," which
Jesus often used of himself, was an acknowledgment of his humanity. But while Jesus was truly human in every respect except for sin
(Heb. 4:15), this phrase is not an indicator of his humanity. Given its
proper context, it is another claim to deity. This is manifest in two
ways: First, the Old Testament messianic use of the phrase "Son of
Man" points to Christ's deity. Daniel writes of the coming Messiah,
"I was watching in the night visions, and behold, One like the Son
of Man, coming with clouds of heaven!" (Dan. 7:13). Second, it is

Jesus's citation of this text that incites the high priest to accuse him of blasphemy. We read, "The high priest said to him, 'I adjure you by the living God, tell us if you are the Christ [Messiah], the Son of God.' Jesus said to him, 'You have said so. But I tell you, hereafter you will see the Son of man seated at the right hand of the Power, and coming on the clouds of heaven.' Then the high priest tore his clothes, and said, 'He has uttered blasphemy'" (Matt. 26:63–65 NRSV). Jesus also uses the term "Son of Man" in the context of his claim to forgive sins, asserting that "the Son of Man has power on earth to forgive sins" (Mark 2:10). He also uses it of his right to judge humankind at his return to earth, affirming, "When the Son of Man comes in His glory, and all the holy angels with Him, then He will sit on the throne of His glory. All the nations will be gathered before Him, and He will separate one from another" (Matt. 25:31–32 NKJV). Likewise Jesus says of his second coming, "Then the sign of the Son of Man will appear in heaven, and then all the tribes of the earth will mourn, and they will see the Son of Man coming on the clouds of heaven with power and great glory" (Matt. 24:30 NKJV). Clearly the phrase "Son of Man" is used here of his deity, as it is in Daniel 7, where he is identified with "the Ancient of Days"—a phrase denoting deity (vv. 9, 13).

The Apologetic Implications

One of the two most important pillars in the Christian apologetic, given the theistic universe and the reliability of the New Testament documents, is Jesus's claim to be God Almighty in human flesh. The other is the miraculous evidence he offered for this claim (see chap. 2), particularly his resurrection from the dead (see chap. 3). In view of the above, the charge that Jesus never really claimed to be God fails completely, as does the futile attempt to take verses out of context to support such a claim.

The claim that Jesus denies he is God. Jesus says to the rich young ruler, "Why call me good? No one is good but God" (Luke 18:19

NRSV). But this is not a denial that he is God; it is a question. Jesus is asking him if he realizes the implications of his statement.

Jesus's statement that "the Father is greater than I" (John 14:28). Neither is this a denial of his deity. The Father as God is greater than Jesus is as a man, and the Father is greater in office but not in nature. Like a human father and son, both Jesus and his Father have the same nature. They differ only in their function.

Jesus's alleged denial of omniscience. Jesus says, "But about that day and hour no one knows, neither the angels in heaven, nor the Son, but only the Father" (Mark 13:32 NRSV). Truly, God does know everything. And Jesus *as God* knows the time of his return. But as the God-Man, Jesus has two natures, and in his human nature Jesus does not know everything. In fact, while on earth he grows in his human knowledge (Luke 2:52).

Jesus is said to be the "firstborn" in creation. Some take this to be a denial of Christ's deity because his apostle says, "He is the image of the invisible God, the firstborn over all creation" (Col. 1:15). But the word *firstborn* can mean priority in rank, not in time, as it clearly does here because he is Creator and Sustainer of all things (vv. 16–17). So Jesus is first *over* creation, not the first *in* creation.

Christ is called "the beginning of the creation of God." In a similar way, critics claim this shows Jesus was the first one created (Rev. 3:14). But here too there is a misunderstanding of the term *beginning.* If Jesus was created, it would contradict the clear teaching that he created all things (John 1:3; Heb. 1:2; Col. 1:16). Further, this same term *beginning* is used of the Lord the Almighty (Rev. 1:8) and the Father who is God (Rev. 21:5–6). So Jesus is the first or *beginning* in the sense that he is the Beginner over of all creations, not the first one made in creation.

The claim to be both God and man is contradictory. Some see a logical problem with claiming that Jesus is both God and man at the same time. This appears to be a violation of the law of noncontradiction. But it is not, because he is not both in the same sense. One can be a father and a husband at the same time but not in the same sense. So Jesus has both a divine and a human nature at the same time but not in the same sense.

Conclusion

Since Jesus's claim to be God is crucial to both the uniqueness and truth of the Christian religion, it is of great apologetic importance to establish his claim to deity. As we have shown, Jesus did this in his discourse in numerous ways, both direct and indirect, because he claimed to be and to do what only God can be and do, including outright claims to be Yahweh, the Great I AM (John 8:58) who revealed himself to Moses. On many occasions those to whom he spoke recognized his claim to be God (Matt. 26:65; Mark 2:10; John 8:59; 10:33). Thus this pillar of Christian apologetics was firmly established by Christ, for in a Jewish monotheistic context (where there is one God exists and miracles are possible), he not only claimed to be God in human flesh but he also proved to be God by numerous supernatural events that supported his claims (see chap. 2).

It is objected that Jesus said to the Father, "that they may know you, the only true God" (John 17:3). This they take to mean that Christ is not God but only the Father is. However, this conclusion does not follow. For it declares that the Father is the only true God, but it does not say that only the Father is God. Indeed, in this very passage the Son is also God with whom he shared an eternal preexistence and glory (v. 5).

7

Jesus's
Apologetic Use of
Prophecy

Jesus is fully conscious of being the fulfillment of Old Testament predictions about the Messiah. Indeed, he says five times that he is the fulfillment of the Old Testament: "Do not think that I came to destroy the Law or the Prophets. I did not come to destroy but to fulfill" (Matt. 5:17 NKJV). After his resurrection, "Beginning at Moses and all the Prophets, [Jesus] expounded to them in all the Scriptures the things concerning Himself" (Luke 24:27 NKJV). He adds later, "All things must be fulfilled which were written in the Law of Moses and the Prophets and the Psalms concerning Me" (Luke 24:44 NKJV). Further, he declares to the Jews, "You search the Scriptures, for in them you think you have eternal life; and these are they which testify of Me" (John 5:39 NKJV). Finally, Jesus says, "Behold, I have come—In the volume of the book it is written of Me—to do Your will, O God" (Heb. 10:7 NKJV). Clearly he is aware of his fulfillment of both Old Testament prophecy and types (see Hebrews 7–10) such as the Passover lamb (see 1 Cor. 5:7).

Jesus's Use of Prophecy as an Apologetic

The Old Testament refers to the apologetic value of prophecy on a number of occasions. Deuteronomy 18 provides a test for a false prophet: "When a prophet speaks in the name of the LORD, if the thing does not happen or come to pass, that is the thing which the LORD has not spoken" (v. 22). In short, an unfulfilled prophecy is indication of a false prophet, of whom Jesus says we should "beware" (Matt. 7:15; see 24:11). Further, the sign of a true prophet is that he or she can unerringly predict the future. The true God says through Isaiah, "For I am God, and there is no other; I am God, and there is none like Me, declaring the end from the beginning. . . . Indeed I have spoken it; I will also bring it to pass. I have purposed it; I will also do it" (Isa. 46:9, 11 NKJV). God says to Isaiah, "Even from the beginning I have declared it to you; Before it came to pass, I proclaimed it to you, Lest you should say, 'My idol has done them'" (Isa. 48:5 NKJV). "Besides Me there is no God. And who can proclaim as I do . . . the things that are coming and shall come?" (Isa. 44:6–7 NKJV). In brief, only God can accurately and repeatedly predict the future, particularly the distant future.

Jesus is aware of the apologetic value of prophecy. After giving his disciples many predictions about the future, he says, "See, I have told you beforehand," implying that this will add to its credibility (Matt. 24:25 NKJV). In John 14:29 he says explicitly, "I have told you before it comes, that when it does come to pass, you may believe" (NKJV).

Jesus's Use of the Old Testament Prophecies about Himself

Jesus is conscious that he is fulfilling Old Testament prophecies about himself; he says so on a number of occasions. Knowing about Zechariah's prediction of a triumphal entry into Jerusalem, he instructs two disciples to get the donkey he will need to ride into the city (Matt. 21:1–3).

> All this was done that it might be fulfilled which was spoken by the prophet, saying:

"Tell the daughter of Zion,
'Behold your King is coming to you,
lowly, and sitting on a donkey.'"

Matthew 21:4–5 NKJV

Even more explicitly, Jesus says of those who came to seize him to crucify him, "But all this was done that the Scriptures of the prophets might be fulfilled" (Matt. 26:56 NKJV).

Of course, there were predictions about Jesus of which he was conscious but over which he had no control. These include what tribe he would come from (Gen. 49:10); whose dynasty he would come from (2 Sam. 7:12–16); in what city he would be born (Micah 5:2), and that he would be born of a virgin (Isa. 7:14). But conscious or not, these prophecies played a significant apologetic role in the life of Christ. Indeed, they were unprecedented and unparalleled, because no other religious leader had any significant, long-range group of predictions that were made hundreds of years in advance and all of which he fulfilled. This is truly supernatural.

Jesus's Personal Prophecies about Himself and Others

In addition to knowing that he was fulfilling Old Testament prophecies, Jesus made predictions about himself, some of which were fulfilled in his lifetime. Others were fulfilled later, and some are yet to be fulfilled at his second coming.

Predictions in Matthew

The Gospel of Matthew alone lists eighty-one predictions, fifty-eight of which are made only by Jesus. Professor Barton Payne notes that "the Gospel of Matthew contains more predictions than any other book of the New Testament, namely 81. Within the whole of Scripture, indeed, the number is exceeded only by the major prophecies of Isaiah and Jeremiah in the OT." Indeed, this is "26% of the [Gospel of Matthew]. A truly high figure for historical narrative."[1] Some of Jesus's fifty-eight predictions recorded by Matthew are:

1. The Word of God will abide forever (5:18).
2. Some unbelievers will protest on judgment day (7:19–23).
3. Abraham, Isaac, and others will be in the kingdom on judgment day (8:11).
4. The day will come when Christ will be taken away (9:15).
5. There will be degrees of punishment on judgment day (10:15).
6. The apostles will be persecuted (10:17–23).
7. Jesus will reunite with the apostles before the preaching tour ends (10:23).
8. Jesus will ascend into heaven (10:32–33).
9. Jesus will die and rise three days later (12:40).
10. There will be a resurrection of believers in the endtime (12:41).
11. The saved will be separated from the unsaved in the endtime (13:30).
12. The kingdom of heaven will experience great growth (13:31–32).
13. The church Christ will build will never be destroyed (16:18).
14. Christ will return in glory with his angels and reward his followers (16:27).
15. The twelve apostles will reign with Christ over the tribes of Israel (19:28).
16. James and John will undergo suffering for Christ (20:23).
17. Christ will be rejected by his people, and the Gentiles will be brought in (21:42–43).
18. There will be a resurrection, and there will be no marriage in heaven (22:30).
19. Jerusalem will reject Christ and become desolate (23:34–38).
20. Jerusalem and the temple will be destroyed (24:22).
21. Mary's act of anointing Jesus will be remembered throughout the world (26:13).
22. Judas, Jesus's betrayer, will be doomed (26:24).
23. Jesus's disciples will flee at his death (26:31).
24. Peter will deny Christ three times (26:34).

Predictions in Mark

Although Mark is a much smaller book than Matthew, it has fifty predictions, which make up 19 percent of his entire book. Of these, Jesus made forty-seven of the predictions, almost all of which are the same as those recorded in Matthew.

Predictions in Luke

Luke's seventy-five predictions make up 22 percent of the narrative. This is second only to Matthew's eighty-one predictions.[2] Twenty-six of these come in the first two chapters before Christ's birth. Most of the rest are made by Christ.

Predictions in John

John contains forty-five predictions. This is 20 percent of the whole book, which is higher than that of Mark. Again, most of the predictions are made by Christ. Since John gives a fresh approach, not following that of the Synoptic Gospels, it contains some predictions not found in Matthew, Mark, or Luke. These include:

1. Jesus has another group of sheep to bring into his fold (10:16).
2. Lazarus will be raised from the dead (11:4, 11, 23, 40).
3. Those who reject Jesus's words will be judged by them in the last day (12:48).
4. The disciples will do greater works than Jesus did (14:12).
5. The Holy Spirit will come and teach the disciples (14:15–26; 16:5–15).
6. The disciples will get a great catch of fish when they cast their net on the other side of the boat (21:6).
7. John will live to an old age (21:18).

Matthew's Record of Fulfillment

Not all prophecy is strictly predictive. Some is typological, awaiting a higher completion in the future. Matthew uses the Greek word *plerao* (fulfill) to mean "fill completely, accomplish, make full, complete, end." He applies it to Christ fifteen times (emphases added):

1. "Now all this was done so that it might be *fulfilled* which was spoken of the Lord by the prophet, saying, Behold, a virgin shall be with child, and shall bring forth a son, and they shall call his name Emmanuel, which being interpreted is, God with us" (Matt. 1:22–23 KJV).
2. "And [Jesus] was there until the death of Herod: that it might be *fulfilled* which was spoken of the Lord by the prophet, saying, Out of Egypt have I called my son" (Matt. 2:15 KJV).
3. "Then was *fulfilled* that which was spoken by Jeremiah the prophet, saying, In Rama was there a voice heard, lamentation, and weeping, and great mourning, Rachel weeping for her children, and would not be comforted, because they are not" (Matt. 2:17–18 KJV).
4. "And he came and dwelt in a city called Nazareth: that it might be *fulfilled* which was spoken by the prophets, He shall be called a Nazarene" (Matt. 2:23 KJV).
5. "That it might be *fulfilled* which was spoken by Esaias [Isaiah] the prophet, saying, The land of Zabulon, and the land of Nephthalim, by the way of the sea, beyond Jordan, Galilee of the Gentiles; The people which sat in darkness saw a great light" (Matt. 4:14–16 KJV).
6. "Think not that I am come to destroy the law, or the prophets: I am not come to destroy, but to *fulfil*" (Matt. 5:17 KJV).
7. "That it might be *fulfilled* which was spoken by Esaias the prophet, saying, Himself took our infirmities, and bare [our] sicknesses" (Matt. 8:17 KJV).
8. "That it might be *fulfilled* which was spoken by Esaias the prophet, saying, Behold my servant, whom I have chosen; my beloved, in whom my soul is well pleased: I will put my spirit upon him, and he shall shew judgment to the Gentiles" (Matt. 12:17–18 KJV).

9. "And in them is *fulfilled* the prophecy of Esaias which saith, By hearing ye shall hear, and shall not understand; and seeing ye shall see and shall not perceive" (Matt. 13:14 KJV).
10. "That it might be *fulfilled* which was spoken by the prophet, saying, I will open my mouth in parables; I will utter things which have been kept secret from the foundation of the world" (Matt. 13:35 KJV).
11. "All this was done that it might be *fulfilled* which was spoken by the prophet, saying, 'Tell the daughter of Zion, "Behold, your King is coming to you, lowly, and sitting on a donkey, a colt, the foal of a donkey"'" (Matt. 21:4–5 NKJV).
12. "But how then shall the scriptures be *fulfilled*, that thus it must be?" (Matt. 26:54 KJV).
13. "But all this was done that the scriptures of the prophets might be *fulfilled*. Then all the disciples forsook him, and fled" (Matt. 26:56 KJV).
14. "Then was *fulfilled* that which was spoken by Jeremy [Jeremiah] the prophet, saying, And they took the thirty pieces of silver, the price of him that was valued, whom they of the children of Israel did value" (Matt. 27:9 KJV).
15. "And they crucified him, and parted his garments, casting lots: that it might be *fulfilled* which was spoken by the prophet, They parted my garments among them, and upon my vesture did they cast lots" (Matt. 27:35 KJV).

Even though these are not all strictly predictive, nonetheless they are anticipatory. Likewise, the Passover lamb looked forward to a future fulfillment of its type in Christ. For Paul says, "Christ, our Passover Lamb, has been sacrificed for us" (1 Cor. 5:7 NLT). In this sense, Christ is the fulfillment of all this kind of Old Testament prophecies.

Old Testament Texts That Are Predictive

Some Old Testament texts are truly predictive. That is, they are specifically about the coming Messiah, and hence, their fulfillment has clear apologetic value. As the above discussion indicates, Jesus is not only aware of these predictions, but as the Messiah, he is also conscious that he is the fulfillment of them. Most, if not all, of the following texts fit into this category.

The prediction that the Messiah will be:

1. *The Seed of the Woman*: "I will put enmity between you [the Serpent] and the woman, and between your seed and her Seed; He shall bruise your head, and you shall bruise His heel" (Gen. 3:15 NKJV).
2. *The Line of Seth*: "And Adam knew his wife again; and she bare a son, and called his name Seth: For God, said she, hath appointed me another seed instead of Abel, whom Cain slew" (Gen. 4:25 KJV).
3. *A Descendent of Shem*: "And he said, Blessed be the LORD God of Shem; and Canaan shall be his servant" (Gen. 9:26 KJV).
4. *The Seed of Abraham*: "I will bless them that bless thee, and curse him that curseth thee: and in thee shall all families of the earth be blessed" (Gen. 12:3 KJV).
5. *Of the Tribe of Judah*: "The scepter shall not depart from Judah, nor a lawgiver from between his feet, until Shiloh come; and unto him shall the gathering of the people be" (Gen. 49:10 KJV).
6. *From the House of David*: "When your days are fulfilled and you rest with your fathers, I will set up your seed after you, who will come from your body, and I will establish his kingdom" (2 Sam. 7:12 NKJV). And, "The days are coming, declares the LORD, when I will raise up to David a righteous branch, a King who will reign wisely and do what is just and right in the land. . . . This is the name by which he will be called: The LORD Our Righteousness" (Jer. 23:5–6).
7. *Conceived of a Virgin*: "Therefore the Lord himself will give you a sign: The virgin will be with child and will give birth to a son, and will call him Immanuel" (Isa. 7:14).

8. *Born in Bethlehem*: "But you, Bethlehem Ephrathah, though you are little among the thousands of Judah, yet out of you shall come forth to Me the One to become Ruler in Israel, whose goings forth are from of old, from everlasting" (Micah 5:2 NKJV).

9. *Killed about AD 33*: "Seventy 'sevens' are decreed for your people and your holy city to finish transgression, to put an end to sin, to atone for wickedness, to bring in everlasting righteousness, and to seal up the vision and prophecy and to anoint the most holy. Know and understand this: From the issuing of the decree to restore and rebuild Jerusalem [444 BC] until the Anointed One [Messiah], the ruler, comes, there will be seven 'sevens,' and sixty-two 'sevens'" (Dan. 9:24–25).[3]

Seven sevens plus sixty-two sevens equal sixty-nine sevens or 483 lunar years of 360 days each by the Jewish lunar calendar. Add to this six more years for the five extra days in our calendar times 483 years, and it makes exactly 483 years (477 + 6) from 444 BC to AD 33. Even by the critics' late date for Daniel (ca. 165 BC) were true, he still foretold the Messiah's death nearly two hundred years in advance of the event. This is an amazing prediction.

10. *Heralded by a Forerunner*: "The voice of one crying in the wilderness: 'Prepare the way of the LORD; Make straight in the desert a highway for our God'" (Isa. 40:3 NKJV).

11. *Proclaimed as King*: "Rejoice greatly, O daughter of Zion! Shout, O daughter of Jerusalem! Behold your king is coming to you; He is just and having salvation, Lowly and riding on a donkey, a colt, the foal of a donkey" (Zech. 9:9 NKJV).

12. *Made to Suffer and Die for Our Sins*: "Surely He has borne our griefs And carried our sorrows: Yet we esteemed Him stricken, smitten by God, and afflicted. But He was wounded for our transgressions, He was bruised for our iniquities; the chastisement of our peace was upon Him, and by His stripes we are healed. . . . The LORD has laid on Him the iniquity of us all. . . . He was led as a lamb to the slaughter. . . . For the

transgressions of My people He was stricken. And they made His grave with the wicked—But with the rich at His death. . . . Yet it pleased the LORD to bruise Him; He has put Him to grief. . . . He bore the sin of many, and made intercession for the transgressors" (Isa. 53:4–10, 12 NKJV).

13. *Pierced in His Side*: "They will look on Me whom they pierced; Yes, they will mourn for Him as one mourns for his only son, and grieve for Him as one grieves for a firstborn" (Zech. 12:10 NKJV).

14. *Raised from the Dead*: "For you will not leave my soul in Sheol, nor will You allow Your Holy One to see corruption. You will show me the path of life" (Ps. 16:10–11 NKJV; cf. Acts 2:30–32). "When You make His soul an offering for sin, He shall see His seed, He shall prolong His days" (Isa. 53:10 NKJV). "The rulers take counsel . . . against His Anointed. . . . Yet I have set My King on My holy hill of Zion. . . . The LORD has said to Me, 'You are My Son, today I have begotten You [from the dead]'" (Ps. 2:2, 6–7 NKJV; cf. Acts 13:33–35).

Conclusion

The use of truly predictive prophecy by Jesus and his disciples in the New Testament places them beyond the realm of reasonable human possibility for several reasons. First, unlike the vague prognostications of Nostradamus, these are specific and verifiable predictions. Second, unlike most psychic predictions, these are numerous, specific, and long-range predictions—made hundreds of years in advance. This places them far above the category of any human prognostications. Take, for example, the psychic predictions made in 1994 about the next year that were 92 percent wrong! Among the failed predictions are:

1. All three news anchors would be replaced.
2. The Queen of England would abdicate.
3. Kathie Lee Gifford would replace Jay Leno.

4. Cindy Crawford would have triplets.
5. Hillary Clinton would plead guilty of shoplifting.
6. Charles Manson would get a sex-change operation.
7. Whitney Houston would marry Mike Tyson.
8. An African plant would cure AIDS.
9. Volcanic action would make a land bridge to Cuba.
10. Madonna would marry Boy George.
11. The Sears Tower in Chicago would lean like the tower of Pisa.
12. A national lottery would cut taxes in half.
13. A teenager would build and detonate a nuclear bomb in South Carolina.
14. Madonna would marry a sheik and become a housewife.
15. Scientists would build a car that runs on tap water.

By comparison to these false prophecies, the numerous, specific, long-range, and highly accurate predictions about Christ's first coming are beyond the realm of human projections.

8

Jesus's
Apologetic Use of
Arguments for God

Jesus lived and taught in a Jewish, theistic culture. Therefore, his audience already presupposed the existence of God, and in this context there was no need for him to provide a rational defense of a theistic worldview. It would be interesting, however, to ask what Jesus would have said to those with a nontheistic worldview. Three sources from which we can make reasonable inferences are: (1) the Old Testament, in which Jesus was thoroughly trained (Luke 2:52; cf. 2 Tim. 3:14–15) and of which he claimed his life and teaching were a fulfillment; (2) the New Testament, which as the inspired product of Jesus's disciples (John 14:26; 16:13) thereby reflects the mind of Christ; and (3) implications in the teachings of Jesus that may be applied to a nontheistic context. When we look at these sources, we find an informative answer as to how Jesus might have responded apologetically to challenges to a theistic worldview.

The Old Testament Response to Nontheism

The main opposition to monotheism in the Old Testament was polytheism, although there are some references to atheism (like Psalm 14:1). As the basis for Jesus's teaching, these Old Testament encounters with nontheistic beliefs provide a basis for understanding how Jesus would have responded to these opposing worldviews.

Jesus was thoroughly instructed in the Old Testament, which is evident from the numerous times he cites it in his teachings as well as in his affirmation: "Do not think that I came to destroy the Law and the Prophets. I did not come to destroy but to fulfill" (Matt. 5:17 NKJV). Likewise, one of his apostles affirms that "what the law could not do in that it was weak through the flesh, God did by sending His own Son in the likeness of sinful flesh, . . . that the righteous requirements of the law might be fulfilled in us" (Rom. 8:3–4 NKJV).

In view of Jesus's dependence on and fulfillment of Old Testament law, it is reasonable to assume that he would have responded the same way to nontheistic worldviews as the writers of Old Testament Scripture, which is filled with attacks on idolatry—the worship of things created by human hands rather than worship of the Creator of the universe. This implies that even though they did not have the Scriptures, pagans should have recognized the Creator from the fact of creation.

Cosmological Argument for God

This is sometimes called the First Cause argument. We know intuitively that every event has a cause. Even the skeptic David Hume never denied this: "I never asserted so absurd a proposition as that anything might arise without a cause."[1] But if every event must have a cause and the universe had a beginning, then it logically follows that there was a cause of the first event or events. Indeed, this is where it starts: "In the beginning God created the heaven and the earth" (Gen. 1:1 NKJV). And it is not surprising that there are some three hundred verses in the Bible referring to the *beginning* of things and life.[2]

Anthropological Argument for God

Within the prophetic challenge to polytheism in the Old Testament is an implicit anthropological argument for God—an argument from human beings to God. For example, the psalmist says, "He who planted the ear, shall He not hear? He who formed the eye, shall He not see?" This implies that every effect not only has a cause but one that is similar to that cause. He then goes on: "He who teaches man knowledge" (Ps. 94:9–10 NKJV). In short, humans can hear, see, and think. Since the cause must be like the effect, there must be a Cause (God) who can hear, see, and think.[3]

Argument for God from the Need to Worship

Isaiah declares in vivid satire the stupidity of worshiping an idol:

> He cuts down cedars for himself. . . .
> He will take some of it and warm himself;
> Yes, he kindles it and bakes bread;
> Indeed he makes a god and worships it;
> He makes a carved image, and falls down to it.
> He burns half of it in the fire. . . .
> He even warms himself. . . .
> And the rest of it he makes into a god,
> His carved image.
> He falls down before it and worships it.
>
> Isaiah 44:14–17 NKJV

Within this powerful imagery of the futility of idolatry is an implied argument for God:

1. Everyone needs to worship something.
2. It is futile to worship something made by humans.
3. Therefore, there really is an unmade Maker who should be worshiped.

It is interesting to note that in this very context of debunking idolatry, the true God reveals himself as Creator. Isaiah writes, "Thus says the LORD . . . who made you and formed you from the womb. . . . I am the LORD, who made all things, who stretched out the heavens alone, who spread out the earth" (Isa. 44:24 RSV). Indeed, those who reject this message are told: "Woe to him who strives with his Maker!" who says, "I have made the earth, and created man on it. I—My hands—stretched out the heavens, and all their host I have commanded" (Isa. 45:9, 12 NKJV). Only a Creator—not another creature—can fulfill the deepest desires of a creature.

Teleological Argument for God

The psalmist cries out: "The heavens declare the glory of God; and the firmament shows his handiwork" (Ps. 19:1 NKJV). Psalm 8 states,

> When I consider your heavens,
>   the work of your fingers,
> the moon and the stars,
>   which you have set in place,
> what is man that you are mindful of him,
>   the son of man that you care for him?
> You made him a little lower than the heavenly beings
>   and crowned him with glory and honor.
> You made him ruler over the works of your hands;
>   you put everything under his feet.
>
> Psalm 8:3–6

Even the famous agnostic Immanuel Kant could not help believing in God. He writes, "Two things fill the mind with ever new and increasing admiration and awe, the oftener and more steadily we reflect on them: the starry heavens above and the moral law within me."[4] Why is this? Because every design has a designer, and the heavens manifest amazing evidence that they are designed. This is called the teleological argument—showing through nature that there must be a God.

Moral Argument for God

The Old Testament offers embryonic forms of the moral argument for God, which affirms that since there is an objective moral law, there must be an objective moral lawgiver. That there is a moral law to which all people are subject—even those who have no form of special revelation—is clear from God's condemnation of pagan nations.

Leviticus 18 is a case in point. God sets forth his moral condemnation of the Canaanites in very forceful words. After condemning sodomy, bestiality, and other forms of immorality, God says to Israel: "Do not defile yourselves with any of these things; for by all these the nations are defiled, which I am casting out before you. For the land is defiled; therefore I visit the punishment of its iniquity upon it, and the land vomits out its inhabitants" (Lev. 18:24–25). So strong was this moral law written on the hearts of the heathen that there was no excuse for their immorality, and God commanded their elimination from the face of the earth!

Existential Argument for God

So deeply ingrained is the instinct for God that the Old Testament calls atheists fools. David says, "The fool has said in his heart, 'There is no God'" (Ps. 14:1 NKJV). His son Solomon, the wisest man who ever lived, observes that a life without God is meaningless: "'Vanity of vanities,' says the Preacher; 'Vanity of vanities, all is vanity'" (Eccles. 1:2 NKJV). The argument for God implied here can be put like this:

1. Whatever human beings really need really exists.
2. Human beings really need God.
3. Therefore, God really exists.

Of course, this does not mean that whatever we want really exists— only what we need. We want a pot of gold at the end of the rainbow, but we really need food and water. It is absurd to believe that if we really need water but some die of thirst, then there is no water anywhere. In the same way, it is absurd to say that if we really need food but some die of hunger, then there is no food anywhere. All of nature rushes to fill a vacuum, so if there is a God-sized vacuum in the human heart, then there must really be a God who can fill it, even though some die without knowing him.

Solomon was one of the wisest and richest men who ever lived, and he tried everything under the sun to satisfy this vacuum in the human heart. He concluded that "all is vanity and vexation of spirit" (Eccles. 1:14 KJV). Apart from God, life is futile. So it is reasonable to assume that Jesus, whose life and ministry were steeped in the Old Testament, would have pointed out the absurdity and meaninglessness of life without God.

Interestingly, even nontheistic philosophers have unwittingly confirmed this thesis. Atheist philosopher Bertrand Russell writes,

> Man is the product of causes which had no prevision of the end they were achieving; that his origin, his growth, his hopes and fears, his loves and his beliefs, are but the outcome of accidental collocations of atoms; that no fire, no heroism, no intensity of thought and feeling, can preserve an individual life beyond the grave; that all the labors of the ages, all the devotion, all the inspiration, all the noonday brightness of human genius, are destined to extinction in the vast death of the solar system, and that the whole temple of man's achievement must inevitably be buried beneath the debris of a universe in ruins.[5]

Russell states the inevitable conclusion of atheism: in spite of the fact that humankind's existence is ultimately meaningless, nonetheless, people must courageously accept this fact and live with this reality haunting them throughout their brief sojourn here on earth.

Not only is life meaningless without God, there is no significance for our existence; humankind exists as another insignificant object in a vast, dark universe headed for extinction. The late atheist astronomer Carl Sagan writes,

> Because of the reflection of sunlight, . . . earth seems to be sitting on a beam of light, as if there were some special significance to this small world. But it's just an accident of geometry and optics. . . . Our posturings, our imagined self-importance, the delusion that we have some privileged position in the Universe, are challenged by this point of pale light. Our planet is a lonely speck in the great enveloping cosmic dark. In our obscurity, in all this vastness, there is no hint that help will come from elsewhere to save us from ourselves.[6]

Sagan, an unbeliever, rightly concludes that if our existence is the result of a cosmic accident, earth and humankind exist simply as a tiny, obscure speck in this gigantic universe. Any idea that our existence has any significance is an illusion that we have created. Therefore, any hope of discovering ultimate meaning and significance should be abandoned.

The New Testament Response to Nontheism

Jesus accepted the Old Testament as the inspired Word of God (Matt. 5:17; John 10:35), so he certainly embraced its example in providing reasons to believe God. Further, the New Testament— written by Jesus's disciples—also indicates the kind of arguments Jesus would have supported in defending the existence of God. Although the apostle Paul was not an earthly disciple of Jesus, nonetheless he was a student of what Jesus taught. Indeed, he cites the words of Jesus on several occasions (Acts 20:35; 1 Cor. 11:23–26; 1 Tim. 5:18). In addition, he received direct instructions from Jesus when he appeared to him on the road to Damascus, as well as from Ananias, from whom Christ commissioned him to receive instructions (Acts 9:3–16). What is more, Paul received direct revelations from Christ as well as being instructed by him three years in Arabia (Gal. 1:12, 17; 2:2). Thus, Paul's epistles are also a reliable source on what Jesus taught.

Cosmological Argument for God

In Acts 17 Paul addresses two groups of unbelievers: Epicureans (atheists) and Stoics (pantheists). The latter believe God is all and the former that there is no God at all. That is, God is everything that exists. To both he has the same message: there is a God who created all. To demonstrate his point, Paul appeals to the fact that there must be a source of the life and breath of all things (Acts 17:25). Further, since we are rational beings, then our cause (our creator) cannot be less than rational (Acts 17:29), for the cause must bear a resemblance to the effects it produces. This is true for the simple reason that a cause cannot produce what it does not possess. Yet "He gives to all life, breath, and all things" (Acts 17:25 NKJV).

Romans 1:19–20 contains the seeds of the cosmological argument for God. Paul writes, "What may be known of God is manifest in them, for God has shown it to them. For since the creation of the world His invisible attributes are clearly seen, being understood by the things that are made, even His eternal power and Godhead, so that they are without excuse" (NKJV). In short, it is evident that there is a Creator because there is a creation that so clearly manifests him that even the pagans "are without excuse." Surely Jesus would agree and would have appealed to such reasoning with those who reject a theistic God.

Further, like the author of Hebrews, Jesus knew that "Every house is built by someone, but He who built all things is God" (Heb. 3:4 NKJV). What is this but a minicosmological argument? As just noted, Jesus knew the world had a *beginning* and that it was a *creation*. But by the same logic that every house has a builder, Jesus knew that the world has a Maker.

Teleological Argument for God

In harmony with the Old Testament, the New Testament informs us that by looking at the design in nature pagans can know there is a God. Paul tells the heathen at Lystra that God "did not leave Himself without a witness, in that He did good, gave us rain from heaven and fruitful seasons, filling our hearts with good and gladness" (Acts 14:17 NKJV). In other words, there must be a God who designed this wonderful world to provide for all our needs.

Moral Argument for God

In Romans 2 the apostle Paul also speaks of the moral law written on the hearts of all people (v. 15). So clear is this law that those who do not heed it will perish (v. 12). But if there is an objective moral law known to all people "by nature" (v. 14), then there must be an objective moral lawgiver. Hence, it is reasonable to conclude that God—the moral lawgiver—exists.

Argument from Existential Need

The New Testament also speaks of the futility of finding happiness in anything less than God himself. Paul warns against trusting riches, noting that "the love of money is a root of all kinds of evil" (1 Tim. 6:10). Further, "We brought nothing into this world, and it is certain we can carry nothing out of it" (v. 7 NKJV). We cannot be content with anything but God, and "godliness with contentment is great gain" (v. 6), but without God everything is loss. This is an abbreviated version of what Solomon teaches in Ecclesiastes 1–2 and what Jesus says in Matthew 6 and Luke 12 (discussed later in this chapter).

Implications from Jesus's Teaching on an Apologetic for Nontheistic Religions

As noted earlier, Jesus had no direct opportunity to interact with nontheistic religious beliefs. But we can infer how he might respond to such viewpoints from his reaction to other forms of unbelief.

Implication for the Cosmological Argument for God

Jesus upholds the basic elements of the First Cause argument. He often references the Genesis creation account (Matt. 19:4–8; Mark

13:19; Luke 11:50). When Jesus is questioned regarding divorce, he develops his position by referring back to the creation account in Genesis 1: "'Haven't you read,' he replied, 'that at the beginning the Creator "made them male and female,"' and said, "For this reason a man will leave his father and mother and be united to his wife, and the two will become one flesh"? So they are no longer two, but one. Therefore what God has joined together, let man not separate'" (Matt. 19:4–6). Jesus points back to the Genesis creation account to defend the covenant of marriage. He believes and teaches that the creation account of Genesis is indeed true, which is why he builds his principles of marriage on it.

In Mark 13:19 Jesus explains what will occur at the end of the age: "Because those will be days of distress unequaled from the beginning, when God created the world, until now—and never to be equaled again." Jesus implicitly sanctions the cosmological argument that if the world had a beginning, then it must have had a beginner. In this verse he asserts that God is that beginner—the one who created the world.

Implication for a Teleological Argument for God

Jesus implies the teleological perspective in speaking about worry—pointing to the order of creation and the Creator's care of his creation.

> Therefore I tell you, do not worry about your life, what you will eat or drink; or about your body, what you will wear. Is not life more important than food, and the body more important than clothes? Look at the birds of the air; they do not sow or reap or store away in barns, and yet your heavenly Father feeds them. Are you not much more valuable than they? Who of you by worrying can add a single hour to his life?
>
> And why do you worry about clothes? See how the lilies of the field grow. They do not labor or spin. Yet I tell you that not even Solomon in all his splendor was dressed like one of these. If that is how God clothes the grass of the field, which is here today and tomorrow is thrown into the fire, will he not much more clothe you, O you of little faith?
>
> Matthew 6:25–30

In teaching against anxiety, Jesus points to creation. He highlights God's care for his creation, which is displayed in his designed order for feeding the animals and his artistic care in the coloring of the lilies. In view of this, Jesus uses the design in creation as evidence for a divine designer.

Implication for a Moral Argument for God

Jesus believes the moral law of God is binding not only on believers but also on unbelievers. He summarizes Moses's law into two parts: First, "Love the Lord your God with all your heart and with all your soul and with all your mind." Second, "Love your neighbor as yourself" (Matt. 22:37, 39). He clarifies our moral duty in one Golden Rule: "Therefore, whatever you want men to do to you, do also to them, for this is the Law and the Prophets" (Matt. 7:12 NKJV).

This is something understood by even unbelievers, which is evident in this statement by Confucius: "Neither do to others what you would not like them to do to you."[7] Jesus also applies the moral law to unbelievers: "If you then, being evil, know how to give good gifts to your children, how much more will your Father who is in heaven give good gifts to those who ask Him" (Matt. 7:11 NKJV). This makes it clear that even evil people know what is "good."

If there is a moral law known to be true by all people, both good and evil, then there must be a moral lawgiver. Thus, Jesus gives tacit approval to the moral argument for God.

Implication for an Existential Argument for God

In this case we do not have to guess what Jesus believes, because he uses this approach in several parables and sayings. He emphasizes that life without God and eternal life is meaningless: "Man does not live on bread alone" (Matt. 4:4). He also affirms emphatically that "one's life does not consist in the abundance of the things he possesses" (Luke 12:15 NKJV). Jesus's half brother James asks, "What is your life? It is even a vapor that appears for a little time and then vanishes away" (James 4:14 NKJV).

If God does not exist, if we are simply an accident of nature, then there is no ultimate purpose for our existence. Each person lives for a brief period in time and then faces annihilation. Furthermore, scientific discoveries show that the universe will run out of energy, reach a state of final entropy, and then cease to exist. That fact forces us to face the questions: What difference will it make that humans or the universe ever existed? What hope can we have in the face of this dismal future? The only certainty is death—the extinction of humans and the universe. In the end, every person will have to conclude that our existence is ultimately meaningless.

Jesus often speaks about the futility of seeking meaning in material riches. For example, "Do not store up for yourselves treasures on earth, where moth and rust destroy, and where thieves break in and steal. But store up for yourselves treasures in heaven, where moth and rust do not destroy, and where thieves do not break in and steal. For where your treasure is, there your heart will be also" (Matt. 6:19–21). Jesus fully understands that material riches can bring temporary happiness, but they cannot provide ultimate joy and meaning in life.

In Matthew 16:26 Jesus states, "What good will it be for a man if he gains the whole world, yet forfeits his soul? Or what can a man give in exchange for his soul?" He teaches that the greatest material gain cannot compare to eternal life with God. He understands that the ultimate meaning in life cannot be found apart from an eternal relationship with the Creator.

In Luke 12:16–21 Jesus tells this parable:

> The ground of a certain rich man produced a good crop. He thought to himself, "What shall I do? I have no place to store my crops." Then he said, "This is what I'll do. I will tear down my barns and build bigger ones, and there I will store all my grain and my goods. And I'll say to myself, 'You have plenty of good things laid up for many years. Take life easy; eat, drink and be merry.'" But God said to him, "You fool! This very night your life will be demanded from you. Then who will get what you have prepared for yourself?" This is how it will be with anyone who stores up things for himself but is not rich toward God.

In this parable, Jesus warns against focusing excessively on or defining one's life in terms of material possessions. In the end, all earthly possessions will be left behind. When this greedy man stands before God and eternity, he will be empty-handed.

In speaking to an atheist, Jesus might echo the lesson of this parable and ask, "What is the ultimate gain from attaining wealth, scientific discovery, or the propagation of the human species? All that is gained in this life will come to an end with the death of humankind and the universe." I believe Jesus would press the atheist to realize the ultimate end of his or her worldview. If there is no God, then our existence is ultimately without meaning, significance, or hope. The dilemma facing humankind is that we cannot live in a world in which our existence is meaningless, which makes it impossible for atheists to consistently live out the implications of their worldview.

Conclusion

Both by the teachings of the Old Testament, which Jesus embraced, and by the New Testament disciples of Christ, who reflected the views of their Master, we can piece together the kinds of arguments Jesus would have used or approved of using in defending theism against nontheism. Further, Jesus left some clear implications of how he would handle such a discussion. What we have found in pursuing these inferences is that Jesus was a rational theist who would have appealed to the cosmological, teleological, and moral arguments for God's existence. Indeed, he also would have agreed with the argument for the existential need for God.

9

Jesus's Alleged Anti-Apologetic Passages

Jesus used reasoned arguments and evidence from prophecy, miracles, and his resurrection to confirm his claims to be the divine Son of God. There were times, however, when Jesus refused to present a defense to support his claims (Matt. 12:38–40; Luke 16:19–31). There were also moments when he appeared to rebuke those who were seeking evidences and reasons for faith (John 20:24–29).

Some believe that since evangelism involves the proclamation of the Word and the work of the Holy Spirit upon the unbeliever, there is no need for apologetics. This position is generally known as fideism. Kenneth Boa writes, "Fideism is an approach to apologetics that argues that the truths of faith cannot and should not be justified rationally. Or, to look at it another way, fideists contend that truths of Christianity are properly apprehended by faith alone."[1] Adherents

129

to this position believe that reason and evidence are not compelling to unbelievers or do not apply to belief in God. One must simply believe.

Was Jesus promoting a fideist approach? Did he desire people to simply believe in him without evidence? If not, then why did he on several occasions refuse to present evidence and sometimes appear to rebuke those who sought reasons to believe? In this chapter, several passages will be studied to respond to these questions. Following these passages from the Gospels, several passages from the Epistles that appear to teach against an apologetic approach will be studied.

Matthew 12:38–40

In Matthew 12:38 the Pharisees and teachers of the law confront Jesus and ask him to perform a "miraculous sign." Jesus rebukes them: "A wicked and adulterous generation asks for a miraculous sign! But none will be given it except the sign of the prophet Jonah" (v. 39).

Some believe that Jesus rebukes the Pharisees because he does not want them to believe in him based on signs but instead to come to him by faith alone. They say Jesus calls these leaders "a wicked and adulterous generation" because they refuse to come to Christ based on faith alone. Those who look for evidence have hearts that are not true to what Christ seeks in his followers; a true believer will not require signs or evidences but will trust the Word of Christ alone.

In order to understand Jesus's response, one must examine the context of this confrontation. First, Matthew records that Christ has already performed numerous miracles (Matt. 4:23–25; 8:1–17, 28–34; 9:1–7, 18–26; 11:20). In fact, this confrontation occurs soon after Jesus heals a man's withered hand (12:9–13) and then delivers a man from demon possession (12:22–23). Jesus has also been teaching and proclaiming God's Word for two years. So these rulers are responding to neither God's Word given through Christ's teachings nor to the numerous miracles he has already performed to confirm his message. Despite all that Jesus has done, the Jewish leaders still demand a sign. Knowing the hardness of their hearts and that they are not asking with an honest intent, Jesus rebukes them, calling them "a wicked and adulterous generation" (12:39).

A biblical principle Jesus exemplifies is that signs are not performed on demand or for those who refuse to believe. Those whose hearts are hardened to the Word of God and the revelation given to them will not believe even if they witness a miracle. Leon Morris states,

> In that they were testing him out (Mark 8:11), it is plain that they did not expect him to come up with anything that would satisfy them. The kind of miracle they were demanding Jesus consistently refused to perform. His miracles were always directed toward the fulfilling of a need felt by those for whom the miracle was performed. Jesus was no circus performer, gratifying the appetite for wonders on the part of people who were not serious about spiritual things. From the beginning he refused to demand that God should do miraculous things for him (Matt. 4:5–7).[2]

Jesus understands the heart condition of his audience and knows that nothing will satisfy their skepticism. They have not responded to the Word of God or the signs already done by Jesus. Jesus refuses to provide a sign except that of Jonah. This sign verifies that he has been sent from God, as was Jonah, and that the judgment of God is upon those who refuse to respond to the message given by God's prophet. D. A. Carson states, "Jesus's 'sign' does not meet the Jews' demand for a special token. Yet it is the only one he will provide. For his own followers, his authority will be grounded in his death and resurrection. And as for those who do not believe, they will only prove themselves more wicked than the Ninevites."[3]

Jesus understands our hearts, and although he does not continue to persuade those who are hard-hearted, he presents evidence to those whose hearts are open to God and the truth. It is not the request for evidence that he rebukes but the corruptness of the heart that lies behind the question.

Luke 16:19–31

The next passage appears in Luke 16. Jesus tells the story of the rich man and a beggar named Lazarus. The rich man suffering in hell begs Abraham to send Lazarus back from the dead to warn his brothers of their impending fate. "Abraham replied, 'They have Moses and the Prophets; let them listen to them.' 'No, father Abraham,' he said, 'but if someone from the dead goes to them, they will repent.' He said to him, 'If they do not listen to Moses and the Prophets, they will not be convinced even if someone rises from the dead'" (vv. 29–31).

From this text some have concluded that signs as well as apologetic evidences are not effective in bringing anyone to faith; the Word of God is all that is needed in evangelism. Neither signs nor apologetic evidences are essential to bring a person to salvation; nonbelievers will be moved by the Word of God as the Holy Spirit anoints them.

To understand Jesus's response, we need to study the entire passage. The story opens with a description of the rich man: "There was a rich man who was dressed in purple and fine linen and lived in luxury every day" (v. 19). He displays his wealth by dressing in an expensive purple outer garment and a fine linen undergarment. William Hendriksen further describes the status of this man: "He was not just rich. He belonged to that class of people to whom the epithet filthy rich is often applied, and not without reason. His living day by day in dazzling splendor marks him as a show-off, a strutting peacock. He wanted everybody to know that he was rich. He was in love . . . with himself."[4]

Living in extravagance, the rich man ignores the needs of Lazarus, who lies in pain and hunger at the gate of the rich man. Lazarus longs "to eat what fell from the rich man's table" (v. 21). The rich man walks past Lazarus daily and is well aware of his plight, but although he apparently has the means to help Lazarus, he coldly ignores his suffering.

Lazarus dies and goes to Abraham's bosom while the rich man dies and is tormented in hell. From hell, the rich man pleads with Abraham to send Lazarus to warn his brothers. He believes that his brothers would listen to someone who had risen from the dead and heed the warning. But Abraham replies, "If they do not listen to Moses and the Prophets, they will not be convinced even if someone rises from the dead" (v. 31).

Only a heart open to God will respond to God's message. No amount of signs can change a heart that is not willing to be challenged by God's Spirit and revelation. Darrell Bock states,

> Those whose hearts are hardened will never accept the call to recognize their need to let God change them. They will not respond to the evidence that God leaves in Jerusalem's empty tomb. Even the great patriarch Abraham testifies to this fundamental truth about sin. In effect, the parable ends by calling the listener not only to believe Jesus but also that great patriarch and custodian of promise, the father of the nation of Israel. To disagree is to reject the testimony of God's servants, stretching back to the patriarch Abraham. To disagree is to challenge divine history.[5]

Miracles confirm God's message and messenger to those whose hearts are open and seeking truth. Those whose hearts are hardened will not respond to God's Word but instead will seek to discredit or explain away any miracles they witness. The rich man in this parable does not respond to God's revealed Word through the law of Moses and the Prophets, which teach that people should honor God by valuing human life and taking care of the poor (e.g., Lev. 19:10; 25:25–46; Deut. 15:4; Isa. 25:4; Amos 2:6–7; Zech. 7:10–11). This rich man saw the plight of Lazarus each day, but his hardness of heart toward God is displayed when he walks by with indifference.

In Matthew 25:31–46 Jesus reveals the judgment that will take place at the end of the age. There he will separate the righteous from the unrighteous—the sheep from the goats. The sheep are identified as those who obeyed God's Word, which is displayed in their care for the poor, the sick, and the imprisoned. The goats are identified by their hardness of heart and disobedience of God's commands. They, like the rich man, did not care for the poor, the sick, and the imprisoned.

Throughout history God has performed great miracles, and yet many still do not come to faith. Exodus records the tremendous miracles God displayed, yet many failed to believe the word of Moses and trust the Lord. As a result, an entire generation—except for Joshua and Caleb—were not allowed to enter the Promised Land. When Jesus raised Lazarus from the dead, many still chose not to believe in him. In fact, the enemies of Christ were even more determined to put him to death (John 11:38–50). Ultimately, even the resurrection of Christ did not produce repentance and faith for those whose hearts were hardened. Miracles confirm the faith of those who honestly seek God with an open heart, but those whose hearts are hardened will not respond to the works of God. That is the lesson revealed in this parable.

Luke 23:8–12

In this passage, Herod comes to examine Jesus, who is on trial before Pontius Pilate. Herod is anxious to see Jesus and hopes "to see him perform some miracle" (v. 8). But Jesus provides no miracles and even remains silent as Herod plies him with many questions.

We can gain an understanding of Herod's character from previous passages in Luke. In Luke 3:19–20 we are introduced to Herod, who has committed adultery and does not repent at John the Baptist's preaching but instead puts John in prison. Later Herod becomes aware of Jesus's activity and hears rumors that possibly John the Baptist has been raised from the dead. Since he was responsible for beheading John the Baptist, Herod wants to see Jesus (Luke 9:7–9). At that point Herod's desire to see him is simply curiosity, but later he seeks to kill Jesus (Luke 13:31).

When Herod finally meets Jesus, he hopes Jesus will perform miracles to entertain him. But it is obvious that Herod's heart is already hardened and unresponsive to the message of God—especially through the preaching of John the Baptist. In the end he shows the state of his heart as he joins his soldiers in mocking Jesus.

Miracles confirm God's message and messenger, but a principle throughout Jesus's ministry is that he will not perform miracles for those whose hearts are hardened to God's message (Luke 11:14–20). Herod wants to be entertained with a miracle, but Jesus is not in the entertainment business.

John 20:24–29

In this passage, ten of the apostles have seen the risen Lord, but Thomas is not among them, and so he remains skeptical. Upon hearing the news from the other disciples, he responds, "Unless I see the nail marks in his hands and put my finger where the nails were, and put my hand into his side, I will not believe it" (v. 25). One week later the apostles are gathered in a room, and Jesus appears to them. Addressing Thomas's unbelief, Jesus says, "Put your finger here; see my hands. Reach out your hand and put it into my side. Stop doubting and believe." Thomas responds, "My Lord and my God" (vv. 27–28). John opens his Gospel with "In the beginning was the Word, and the Word was with God, and the Word was God" and culminates with Thomas's confession that Jesus is "My Lord and my God" (John 1:1; 20:28).

Jesus's response to Thomas is, "Because you have seen me, you have believed; blessed are those who have not seen and yet have believed" (John 20:29). Many take his response to Thomas as a rebuke, concluding that the true faith Christ desires from his followers is faith that is not based on evidence. But this is not a rebuke but rather an acknowledgment of Thomas's declaration of faith. D. A. Carson states, "It is better to understand the first part of Jesus's response as a statement (and to that extent a confirmation of Thomas's faith)— one that prepares the way for the beatitude that follows: blessed are those who have not seen and yet have believed."[6]

Jesus refuses to present evidence to the hard-hearted Pharisees (Matt. 12:38–39), but he responds to Thomas's request because he is open to God and seeking the truth. When he sees Jesus and believes, Jesus acknowledges Thomas's declaration of faith. Then he points to a future time when he will ascend to his Father in heaven and people will not have the advantage the disciples had of seeing the tangible evidence of his presence. Jesus concludes the encounter not with a rebuke to Thomas but by pronouncing a blessing upon those believers who will follow him without any direct physical evidence but by relying on the words and witness of the apostles.

Romans 8:16

In addition to the misinterpretation of Jesus's words by opponents of apologetics, several things his disciples said are misunderstood by some fideists. These are also used to claim that the Bible is opposed to apologetics.

Romans 8:16 states, "The Spirit himself testifies with our spirit that we are God's children." Some interpret this verse to mean that only the work of the Holy Spirit can save an individual. Apologetics is ineffective in leading an unbeliever to Christ because salvation is the result solely of the Holy Spirit moving in a person's spirit as the individual encounters the gospel.

To understand this verse, we must look at the context. Chapter 8 begins with a confirmation to believers: "Therefore, there is now no condemnation for those who are in Christ Jesus" (v. 1). They are no longer under the judgment of God. After declaring that believers are justified before God, Paul then emphasizes the indwelling and work of the Holy Spirit.

First, the Holy Spirit regenerates a person to new life and sets him or her free from the law of sin and death (v. 2). Paul then explains how this is accomplished. This victory cannot be attained through the law because of the weakness of the flesh; instead, God through his Son fulfills the law (vv. 3–4).

Second, Paul displays the contrast between the sinful nature and the nature of the individual indwelt by the Spirit (vv. 5–8). The sinful mind focuses on the desires of the flesh, is hostile to God, and does not live in obedience to God. In contrast, the Spirit-filled individual focuses on what God desires, experiences life and peace, and lives in obedience to God.

Third, the Holy Spirit empowers the believer to live a holy life, which was not possible before salvation in Christ (vv. 9–14). Believers no longer have to live according to the sinful nature; instead, the Spirit empowers them to live a life that is pleasing to God.

Fourth, the Holy Spirit assures believers of their status as children of God and coheirs with Christ (vv. 15–17). Not only do Christians have the assurance from the Word of God, but the Holy Spirit also confirms in our spirit that we are God's children. Verse 16 addresses the assurance of the present and future status of the believer. A person who comes to faith is freed from sin, empowered to live a new life, and assured of his or her future inheritance.

This passage does not negate the need for apologetics. Unbelievers need to be given a presentation of the gospel that includes compelling evidence for the truth of the Christian message. Through this evidence the Holy Spirit can work on their heart or will to accept Christ in their life. Once they put their faith in Christ, the "Spirit himself testifies with our spirit" that we are in Christ and secure in our future inheritance (v. 16). Evidence of one's salvation is a life of obedience to Christ (John 14:15; Rom. 8:9) and the inner witness of the Holy Spirit, who bears fruit in our life by our good works (James 2:14–26).

1 Corinthians 1:20–21

First Corinthians 1:21 states, "For since in the wisdom of God the world through its wisdom did not know him, God was pleased through the foolishness of what was preached to save those who believe." Some interpret this passage as meaning that evangelism involves the straightforward preaching of the gospel and the anointing of the Holy Spirit without the use of reason or evidence. They insist that the human wisdom or reason employed by apologetics cannot bring unbelievers to a saving knowledge of God. Instead, Christians should simply preach the gospel and allow the Holy Spirit to work on the hearts of unbelievers.

Careful examination of this passage in context, however, does not support such an anti-apologetic interpretation. It does not teach that fallen people cannot comprehend the evidence for God nor that they are unable to understand truth about God. According to Romans 1:19–20, unbelievers who look at the created order can clearly see that God exists, and they can know several of his invisible qualities. Paul says that for this reason, even those who have not heard the gospel are without excuse.

But 1 Corinthians 1:21 does not deal with the existence of God or the evidence for Christ. Rather, it focuses on God's plan of salvation—the cross of Christ—which cannot be known by human reason alone but must be revealed by God through divine revelation. Fallen people think according to worldly wisdom, which exalts self, pride, and ego. The gospel presents a message that is contrary to the values and wisdom of the world; it preaches humility and self-sacrifice exemplified by the Son of God on the cross. Since the wisdom of the world is contrary to God's wisdom, fallen men and women in all their intellect cannot come to know God's salvation plan on their own, and they regard the message of the cross as foolishness. The idea of God coming in humility as a servant to die on the cross for humankind is foreign to worldly thinking. It is not that the message cannot be apprehended but that it is contrary to a sinful person's thinking.

Paul's statement also should not be taken as grounds for anti-intellectualism. In this passage he criticizes worldly wisdom—a common theme in his letters and other Epistles (James 3:13–18; 1 John 2:15–17). Paul and other inspired writers exhort believers to stand against worldly wisdom but instead seek after godly wisdom (Prov. 1; Rom. 12:1–2; 1 Cor. 2:6–16; James 1:5). Christian apologetics stands for truth, upholds God's Word, and exalts Christ in the pursuit of godly wisdom rather than worldly wisdom.

But the Christian apologist must understand the role of apologetics. Craig Blomberg states, "Compelling arguments for the faith must always be formulated, but only the convicting work of the Spirit will ever use them to bring people to Christ."[7] Through exposing the fallacies of worldly wisdom and presenting compelling arguments for the truth of Christianity, apologetics may cause an individual to see the fallacy of his or her beliefs and the evidence for Christianity. But this person may still reject Christianity because of his or her pride. It is only as the Holy Spirit works through these arguments and evidences that a person's heart is moved to receive Christ. As the believer matures in the Lord, the Holy Spirit through the Word of God renews the mind from worldly thinking to the mind of Christ (Rom. 12:1–2).

1 Corinthians 2:2–5

Paul says, "For I resolved to know nothing while I was with you except Jesus Christ and him crucified. I came to you in weakness and fear, and with much trembling. My message and my preaching were not with wise and persuasive words, but with a demonstration of the Spirit's power, so that your faith might not rest on men's wisdom, but on God's power."

This passage is interpreted by some as teaching that all that is needed is a presentation of the gospel. The use of reason and evidence is equivalent to relying on "men's wisdom." Because Paul states that he "resolved to know nothing . . . except Jesus Christ and him crucified," they believe the Christian should rely solely on the gospel and the Word of God.

Some think Paul wrote this after his experience with the Athenian philosophers (Acts 17:16–34). They think Paul believed his experience in Athens was a failure and so he decided to change his strategy or return to a former approach of only preaching the gospel of Christ crucified.[8] Reasoned arguments and evidence are a hindrance and not essential in evangelism.

There are several reasons this passage should not be understood as teaching against apologetics. Paul's experience in Athens was not a failure. Several people became followers of Christ, including Dionysius, a key individual who was a member of the Areopagus

(v. 34) and whom church tradition teaches became the first bishop of Athens.[9] When Paul states that he "resolved to know nothing" (1 Cor. 2:2), he did not mean that he is leaving all other knowledge aside to focus only on the message of the gospel.[10]

Paul then reminds the Corinthians that he is not an articulate preacher, so his message does not come with the eloquence or persuasive words that are the hallmark of the Sophist philosophers. Instead, Paul's message is centered on Christ as the only way to eternal life. An unbeliever coming to faith is accomplished by the power of the Holy Spirit and cannot be attributed to the work of humans.

The fact that Paul focuses on the message of the cross does not mean, however, that he did not engage in apologetics. In Philippians 1:16 Paul states that he is appointed for the "defense of the gospel," and in 1 Corinthians 15 he presents an apologetic message for the resurrection of Christ. He imparts his case in a well-reasoned fashion, presenting the evidence of prophecy from the Scriptures and providing a list of witnesses, specifically identifying several. Also, when Paul stands before King Agrippa, he presents an apologetic defense of his ministry (Acts 26), pointing to evidence from the Old Testament and his own experience, as well as appealing to witnesses and facts of which Agrippa is aware.

Therefore, the appropriate interpretation of 1 Corinthians 2:2–5 is not that Paul is teaching against the use of apologetics but that his focus is on the gospel message. He does not rely on eloquent speech but rather on the Holy Spirit to bring people to Christ. Paul's use of reasoned arguments and evidence in his presentations shows that apologetics is a key component of his message to an unbelieving world.

1 Corinthians 2:14

First Corinthians 2:14 states, "The man without the Spirit does not accept the things that come from the Spirit of God, for they are foolishness to him, and he cannot understand them, because they are spiritually discerned." Some misinterpret this passage as teaching that only an act of the Holy Spirit enables unbelievers to perceive truth about God; therefore, salvation comes through an act of the Holy Spirit. Apologetics does little for an unbeliever who cannot comprehend spiritual truths.

Paul's theme in 1 Corinthians 2:6–16 is that worldly wisdom opposes the knowledge of God but wisdom that is beneficial is consistent with biblical teaching. He develops this point by contrasting believers with unbelievers in a section that parallels a previous passage from 1 Corinthians 1:18–25.

Paul begins 1 Corinthians 2:6–10 by stating that God's wisdom is received by believers but rejected by unbelievers. Then he elaborates by contrasting believers, who have the Spirit, and unbelievers, who do not have the Spirit (vv. 10–16), using a syllogism to support his point.

> The Spirit searches all things, even the deep things of God. For who among men knows the thoughts of a man except the man's spirit within him? In the same way no one knows the thoughts of God except the Spirit of God. We have not received the spirit of the world but the Spirit who is from God, that we may understand what God has freely given us.
>
> 1 Corinthians 2:10–12

Paul's first premise is that only a person's spirit can know another individual's thoughts; therefore only the Holy Spirit can know the thoughts of God. The second premise is that Christians have the Spirit of God. The logical conclusion is that Christians can understand the thoughts of God that he chooses to reveal (v. 13).

Then in verse 14 Paul presents three descriptions of people without the Spirit (the Greek word used here is *psychikos*). First, "The man without the Spirit does not accept the things that come from the Spirit of God." The term *accept* is the Greek word *dekomai*, which means to receive, take, or welcome.[11] One who *accepts* receives an offer deliberately and readily.[12] In this case the individual receives the truths from God with a favorable attitude.[13]

People without the Spirit do not receive or welcome the spiritual truths from God—not because they do not perceive or understand these truths but because they reject them. Gordon Fee writes, "The implication is not that *psychikos* persons are simply incapable of understanding things of the Spirit, but that, because of their being 'merely human' (i.e., without help of the Spirit), they 'reject' the things of the Spirit."[14]

Second, people without the Spirit regard the things of the Spirit as foolishness (see 1 Cor. 1:18–24). That is, they are silly to them. God's teachings are contrary to an unsaved individual's thinking and values.

Third, Paul states that the unsaved individual does not welcome spiritual truths from God. He is not saying that unbelievers are unable to apprehend spiritual truths. They *perceive* the truth, but they are not willing to *receive* it (Rom. 1:20). In fact, many non-Christians can masterfully exegete a biblical text. What Paul means in 1 Corinthians 2:14 is that those without the Spirit cannot attain the full understanding of the text.

There are several nuances of the word *understand* (*ginowsko*). The one Paul is most likely referring to is the full knowledge that is gained through experience.[15] Blomberg writes, "The 'understand' these non-Christians do not possess is what the Bible consistently considers to be the fullest kind of understanding: a willingness to act on and obey the Word of God."[16] Unbelievers are hindered from a full understanding because God's truths are meant not only to be studied but to be obeyed and applied (see Matt. 7:24–27; James 1:22). Unbelievers lack the experiential knowledge of God because they have not received his forgiveness and experienced his transforming power. Once again the issue is not the mind's inability to understand the gospel or to know basic truths of God. The issue that keeps unbelievers from coming to Christ is the will; they choose to reject God's truth. God can use Christian apologetics to remove intellectual roadblocks and confront people with their need to surrender their life to Christ. But then the Holy Spirit must move in their heart.

Ephesians 2:1

In Ephesians 2 Paul describes the state of the individual before experiencing the transforming and renewing work of Christ: "As for you, you were dead in your transgressions and sins" (v. 1). The word *dead* in this passage refers to an individual's spiritual state before Christ. The unsaved person is spiritually dead, meaning that he or she is without spiritual life and is therefore separated from God.[17]

There are some scholars who exaggerate the noetic effects of sin on fallen humans. They interpret this verse to mean that sin has influenced our reasoning capabilities so that we are unable to understand spiritual truth and are therefore unable to respond to God. If this is the case, using reasoned arguments (as apologists do) is a futile effort because fallen people do not have the ability to understand the truths being presented nor can they respond positively to the presentation of the evidence.

Although the word *dead* means that unsaved individuals are separated from God, it does not imply that the image of God in them has been completely obliterated so that they cannot understand spiritual truth. Spiritually dead people are still able to comprehend and respond to spiritual truth. Romans 1:20 states, "For since the creation of the world God's invisible qualities—his eternal power and divine nature—have been *clearly seen*, being understood from what has been made, so that men are without excuse" (emphasis added). God is just in judging all people, because even fallen men and women have not lost their reasoning capabilities, and they understand facets of God's character and truth from the created order. Unbelievers can know truth about God but still refuse to acknowledge and respond to that truth. Even after Adam and Eve's fall in the Garden of Eden, they could still communicate with and respond to God (Gen. 3:9–10).

These texts indicate that the image of God in humans is corrupted but not destroyed by sin—it is effaced but not erased, corrupted but not annihilated. The faculties in humans that are part of the image of God are not destroyed; however, they are not capable of attaining or initiating salvation on their own.[18] Since fallen people have the ability to reason and discern truth, apologetics is valid and necessary to address the questions and challenges an unsaved person may present. Through a clear presentation of reasons and evidence, that individual might come to understand that Christianity is true.

Hebrews 11:6

Hebrews 11:6 states, "And without faith it is impossible to please God, because anyone who comes to him must believe that he exists and that he rewards those who earnestly seek him." Some take this verse to mean that belief in God is purely an act of faith not built on evidence but essentially an act of the will. They claim their conclusion is also supported by verse 1: "Faith is being sure of what we hope for and certain of what we do not see."

In order to properly understand this passage, we must look at the previous chapter. There the writer to the Hebrews exhorts his readers to persevere in the faith. They are suffering persecution and hardship, including confiscation of property and imprisonment (Heb. 10:34), but they are able to persevere in difficulty because of the future hope of an eternal reward (vv. 34–35). The believers do not see tangible evidence of this future hope, but they can have a steadfast faith based on the character of God.

How do they know that God is faithful to his Word and can be trusted? The writer points to the record of God's faithfulness to saints in the past as evidence upon which they can build their faith. Verses 26–30 also remind the readers that God judges those who deliberately sin and disobey his Word.

Based on the history of God's actions, believers can have faith in the Lord and obey and trust him even though they may not see tangible results or the future blessings promised. Hebrews 11 is a reminder of the many men and women of Old Testament times who were faithful even though they had only the promise of God to rest upon without any visible evidence that the promises made to them would be fulfilled. F. F. Bruce says,

The promises related to a state of affairs belonging to the future; but these people acted as if that state of affairs were already present, so convinced were they that God could and would fulfill what he had promised. Their faith consisted simply in taking God at his word and directing their lives accordingly; things yet future as far as their experience went were thus present to faith and things outwardly unseen were visible to the inward eye.[19]

The faith described here is the hope God's people had in the future fulfillment of his promises to them even though they could not tangibly see the fulfillment of the promises. Those believers knew they could trust God because of the evidence of his past record of faithfulness to his Word. The author of Hebrews lists examples of men and women who displayed such faith in the future promises of God. Abel offered a better sacrifice than Cain. Enoch was translated to heaven because of his faith. Noah built his ark before the flood even though he had not seen rain (vv. 4–5, 7).

The faith spoken of in verse 6 refers to the belief in the invisible spiritual order and in the promises of God that have not yet been fulfilled. Belief in the spiritual order begins with belief in the existence of God—not a belief that a God exists but a belief that the God of faithfulness revealed in the Scriptures exists. Those who have this faith can approach God with confidence, knowing he is faithful to reward those who truly seek him. So in this context believers cannot please God without faith—belief in his faithfulness and willing patience as they await the promised reward.[20]

In addition, the faith described in this passage is built on the past record of God, who has shown himself to be faithful and who will continue to act in faithfulness to his promises. God is pleased not by blind trust without evidence but by faith built on evidence from history that gives believers confidence to wait patiently on God for the fulfillment of future promises. Hebrews 11:6 does not speak against apologetics but instead teaches that faith in Christ comes as an act of trust based on the evidence that confirms him to be the Son of God.

Conclusion

These passages teach us that Jesus, as well as his disciples, under-stood not only how but also when to use apologetics. In the same way, the apologist today must understand how and when to use evidence when engaging an unbeliever. Evidence by itself does not bring anyone to faith. If the person displays a hardened heart and is unwilling to evaluate the evidence, he or she is resisting the Holy Spirit and will not be persuaded (Acts 7:51). Jesus said he wanted to bring the Jews into the fold but they "were not willing" (Matt. 23:37). Apologetics can bring the unbeliever to intellectual ascent, but only the Holy Spirit can persuade a person to change his or her heart and will.

There comes a point in the process when the Christian apologist must deal with the heart issue of the unbelieving person. If the individual is unwilling to consider the evidence, the believer should consider other reasons for unbelief. Perhaps it is due to bad personal experiences with Christians, lifestyle issues, or pride.

There comes a time when the Christian must decide to follow Jesus's admonition: "Do not give what is holy to the dogs; nor cast your pearls before swine, lest they trample them under their feet" (Matt. 7:6 NKJV). As Solomon says, "Do not answer a fool according to his folly, or you will be like him yourself" (Prov. 26:4). When an unbeliever's questions or attitude reveal that he or she is looking for excuses not to face the issues rather than honestly seeking answers, the apologist should point this out and end the discussion. The issue is not the evidence but the hard-heartedness of the unbeliever. It is time to move on and save one's time and energy for another person, praying that God's Spirit will work on the heart of this individual.

10

Jesus's Life
as an
Apologetic

Jesus not only had an apologetic, he was an apologetic. When his opponents said, "Now we know that You have a demon" (John 8:41, 52 NKJV), Jesus's answer is straight and to the point: "Which of you convicts Me of sin?" (v. 46 NKJV). In short, the evidence of Jesus's impeccable life demonstrates that his testimony is true.

Jesus offered numerous witnesses to the truth of what he taught, including the testimony of the Old Testament, Abraham, Moses, and his heavenly Father (see chap. 1); his miracles (chap. 2); his resurrection (chap. 3); and his fulfillment of prophecy (chap. 7). But one of the most powerful and most neglected testimonies is that of his sinless life.

Jesus Was Completely Human

As a backdrop for understanding the apologetic value of Jesus's superlative character, we need to remember that he was completely human. He had a human mother, a human prenatal life, a human childhood, a human adulthood, human relatives, human friends, human emotions, and a human death.

Jesus's Human Mother

His mother, Mary, was a human being with a human ancestry (Luke 3:23–38) and a human cousin named Elizabeth (Luke 1:36). Mary went through a normal nine-month human pregnancy (Luke 1:36; 2:5–7), and she had a human delivery of her child as she "brought forth her firstborn Son" (Matt. 1:25 NKJV). She also had normal human anxieties (Luke 2:44–45, 48), and she had other human children (Mark 6:3). Mary attended human social events such as a wedding (John 2:1) and religious events such as the circumcision and the dedication of her child (Luke 2:22–23).

Jesus's Human Prenatal Life

Jesus began as a conceptus, grew into an embryo, and went through all the human development that a normal human fetus undergoes. In accord with a modern science understanding, Jesus's heart muscle began to pulsate twenty-one days after conception, his first brain wave occurred forty-two days after conception, and by the third month he could feel organic pain and even suck his thumb. A couple months later he was dreaming and swimming in his mother's womb, just like other human babies.

Jesus's Human Childhood

Like other Jewish children, Jesus was circumcised on the eighth day and dedicated in the temple when he was forty days old (Luke 2:21–24). He ate, drank, and exercised as he grew physically like other children, and he also grew in understanding (v. 52). Jesus even obeyed his parents, like any other human child should (v. 51). Although there are apocryphal stories of childhood miracles, they were not recorded until the second and third centuries; Jesus's first miracle was as an adult when he turned water into wine (John 2:1–11).

Jesus's Human Adulthood

Jesus also had a completely human adulthood. Like anyone else, he became hungry (Matt. 4:2), thirsty (John 4:7; 19:28), and even physically tired (John 4:6). He went to social events (Luke 7:34, 36; John 2:2), as normal human beings do. The devil tempted him to sin, as he also tempts other humans (Matt. 4:1; Heb. 4:15). Jesus also at times grew weary of the crowd and had to withdraw for rest (Mark 6:31). He was so human that he even cried over a friend's death (John 11:35).

Jesus's Human Relatives

The record shows that Jesus had siblings. When he taught in his hometown synagogue, the people said, "Is this not the carpenter, the Son of Mary, and brother of James, Joses, Judah, and Simon? And are not His sisters here with us?" (Mark 6:3 NKJV). Before his resurrection "even his own brothers did not believe in him" (John 7:5). And at one point "His own people . . . went out to lay hold of Him, for they said, 'He is out of His mind'" (Mark 3:21 NKJV). After his resurrection Jesus was seen by his half brother James (1 Cor. 15:6–7), who was converted and later became one of the "pillars" of the church (Gal. 2:9). James and Jude, another of Jesus's half brothers, each wrote an epistle (James 1:1; Jude 1).

Jesus's Human Friends

"Now Jesus loved Martha and her sister [Mary] and Lazarus" (John 11:5 NKJV), at whose house he stayed many times. His special friendship is expressed in Mary's words, "Lord, behold, he whom You love is sick" (John 11:3 NKJV), as well as his tears for Lazarus when he died (John 11:35).

Jesus's Human Emotions

Jesus experienced a full range of human emotions. When he saw Mary crying over her brother's death, Jesus "groaned in the spirit and was troubled" (John 11:33 NKJV). He was angered by hypocrisy, declaring: "Woe unto you scribes and Pharisees, hypocrites!" (Matt. 23:29 KJV). Weeping over Jerusalem, he cried out, "O Jerusalem, Jerusalem, the one who kills the prophets. . . . How often I wanted to gather your children together, as a hen gathers her chicks under her wings, but you were not willing!" (Matt. 23:37 NKJV). He agonized in the Garden of Gethsemane, and "His sweat became like great drops of blood" (Luke 22:44 NKJV). He even had "vehement cries and tears" (Heb. 5:7). On the cross Jesus felt forsaken by his Father and cried, "My God, my God, why have you forsaken me?" (Matt. 27:46).

Jesus's Human Death

Unlike the sons of Adam (Rom. 5:12), Jesus was not intrinsically mortal, but he died a human death. Indeed, he suffered before he died (1 Peter 3:18 NKJV), being "a Man of sorrows and acquainted with grief" (Isa. 53:3 NKJV). He was also "put to death in the flesh" (1 Peter 3:18 NKJV) that "he might taste death for everyone" (Heb. 2:9). In short, Jesus was just as human as any other person except that he was without sin (Heb. 4:15). Yet before the fall Adam was also sinless (Gen. 1:26–2:25) even though he was completely human, and we will be sinless in heaven (Rev. 21:4).

Contrary to the early heresies called Docetism, which denied his humanity completely, and Apollinarism, which diminished it, Jesus was 100 percent human. Even the early Christian creeds affirm Jesus's humanity. The Apostles' Creed (second century AD) declares that he "was conceived of the Holy Spirit, born of the Virgin Mary, suffered under Pontius Pilate, was crucified, died, and was buried"—all of which express his true humanness. The Nicene Creed (AD 325) affirms that he "was incarnate of the Holy Spirit and the Virgin Mary and became truly human." The Chalcedonian Creed (AD 451) adds, "This selfsame one is perfect both in deity and in humanness . . . [and] was born of Mary the virgin, who is God-bearer in respect of his humanness."

Jesus Was Completely Sinless

Knowing that Christ was thoroughly and utterly human in every respect makes his sinlessness all the more amazing. His impeccable character is confirmed by his contemporaries—both friend and foe.

Jesus's Sinlessness and Flawless Character Confirmed

The apostles of Christ affirmed his sinlessness. The writer of Hebrews, who knew the twelve apostles (Heb. 2:3–4), declares, "We have one who has been tempted in every way, just as we are—yet was without sin" (Heb. 4:15). Peter, a leader among the twelve apostles, says, "Christ [is] a lamb without blemish or defect. . . . He committed no sin, and no deceit was found in his mouth. . . . For Christ died for sins once for all, the righteous for the unrighteous" (1 Peter 1:19; 2:22; 3:18). John, Jesus's beloved disciple, says that he is righteous and pure (1 John 2:29; 3:3). The apostle Paul asserts that "God made him [Jesus] who had no sin to be sin for us" (2 Cor. 5:21).

Jesus challenges his enemies, "Which of you convicts Me of sin?" (John 8:46 NKJV), but even they cannot find a flaw in his character. Judas, his betrayer, confesses, "I have sinned by betraying innocent blood" (Matt. 27:4 NKJV). Governor Pilate, who presides at Jesus's trial, declares, "I am innocent of the blood of this just Person" (Matt. 27:24 NKJV). And Pilate's wife advises him, "Have nothing to do with that just Man" (Matt. 27:19 NKJV).

A centurion who helped crucify Jesus exclaims, "Certainly this was a righteous Man!" (Luke 23:47 NKJV; see also Matt. 27:54). The thief on the cross is so impressed by Jesus that he requests, "Jesus, remember me when you come into your kingdom" (Luke 23:42). Even the Herodians who oppose Jesus admit, "Teacher, . . . we know you are a man of integrity and that you teach the way of God in accordance with the truth. You aren't swayed by men, because you pay no attention to who they are" (Matt. 22:16).

The Testimony of Jesus's False Accusers

During his earthly ministry, many false accusations are made against Jesus. The Pharisees attack his character: "This fellow does not cast out demons except by Beelzebub, the ruler of the demons" (Matt. 12:24 NKJV). But this is an indirect admission of Jesus's supernatural power because their attack is in response to his healing a demon-possessed, mute, and blind man.

When Jesus is betrayed by Judas and then brought before the Sanhedrin, even the false witnesses indirectly testify to Jesus's unblemished character. The best they can come up with is hardly a negative; they repeat Jesus's prophecy that he "will destroy this man-made temple and in three days will build another, not made by man" (Mark 14:58). The Jewish high priest charges, "You have heard the blasphemy [that he claims to be the Christ, the Son of God]! What do you think? And they all [the Sanhedrin] condemned him to be worthy of death" (Mark 14:64). But Jesus has already proved by his miracles and will verify by his resurrection that he is the Son of God he claims to be. This is hardly a flaw in his character.

The Jewish leaders at Jesus's trial claim: "We found this fellow perverting the nation, and forbidding to pay taxes to Caesar, saying that He Himself is Christ, a King" (Luke 23:2 NKJV). But Jesus hardly subverted the nation when he told the people, "Render therefore unto Caesar the things which are Caesar's" (Matt. 22:21 KJV). In addition, he did pay taxes (Matt. 17:24–27), and he submits peacefully to the authority of Rome to crucify him unjustly. Finally, at the cross the passersby mock him: "Aha! You who destroy the temple and build it in three days, save Yourself, and come down from the cross!" (Mark 15:29–30 NKJV). But this is indirect testimony to his claim to and proof of his deity because it refers to his death and resurrection (John 2:19–21).

So even false accusers attest to Jesus's flawless character. No one successfully meets his challenge to accuse him of sin (John 8:46). In addition, what we know of Christ's enemies outside the New Testament does not contradict what we have from his direct contemporaries.

The Testimony of Extrabiblical Sources to the Character of Christ

There are numerous early non-Christian sources with references to Jesus and his disciples. They give us a view from a distance of what early non-Christians thought of Jesus's character and teaching.

Tacitus—This first-century Roman historian speaks of

Christus [Christ], from whom the name [Christian] had its origin, suffered the extreme penalty during the reign of Tiberius at the hands of one of our procurators, Pontius Pilatus, and a most mischievous superstition, thus checked for the moment, again broke out not only in Judaea, the first source of the evil, but even in Rome, where all things hideous and shameful from every part of the world find their centre and become popular.[1]

The charge of a "mischievous superstition" and "evil" is understandable, since Jesus was heralded a "king of the Jews," which could be mistakenly perceived as a threat to the Roman king. But the charge that Christianity is "mischievous superstition" is hardly morally culpable. Indeed, it may be an indirect reference to Jesus's resurrection, which would be a confirmation that he is the sinless Son of God.

Suetonius—A Roman historian and the chief secretary of Emperor Hadrian (AD 69–after 122), Suetonius makes two references to Christ. First, "Because the Jews at Rome caused continuous disturbances at the instigation of Chrestus, he expelled them from the city." Second, "After the great fire at Rome . . . punishments were also inflicted on the Christians, a sect professing a new and mischievous religious belief."[2] This tells us little or nothing directly about Jesus's character and more about how Rome viewed any challenge to its authority, but Suetonius does confirm the existence of Christ Jesus.

Josephus—Flavius Josephus (ca. AD 37/38–97) was a Jewish historian working under the auspices of Roman Emperor Vespasian. Josephus's *Antiquities of the Jews* (ca. AD 90–95) contains two passages of interest. The first refers to James, "the brother of Jesus, who was called Christ."[3] This tells us nothing directly about Christ's character, but a second reference is more explicit: "Now there was about this time Jesus, a wise man, if it be lawful to call him a man. For he was one who wrought surprising feats. . . . He was [the] Christ . . . He appeared to them alive again the third day, as the divine prophets had foretold these and ten thousand other wonderful things concerning him."[4]

The genuineness of the latter passage has been questioned by many who doubt that Josephus, a Jew, would have said that Jesus was the

Jewish Messiah who rose from the dead. Indeed, Origen claims that Josephus did not believe Jesus was the Messiah.[5] Despite these concerns, there are several reasons in favor of accepting the other part of the text (except for "he was Christ") as genuine.[6] Finally, an Arabic version of the text probably contains the basic elements of Josephus's original version without the questionable parts. It reads as follows:

> At this time there was a wise man named Jesus. His conduct was good and (he) was known to be virtuous. And many people from among the Jews and the other nations became his disciples. Pilate condemned him to be crucified and to die. But those who had become his disciples did not abandon his discipleship. They reported that he had appeared to them three days after his crucifixion, and that he was alive; accordingly he was perhaps the Messiah, concerning whom the prophets have recounted wonders.[7]

What makes the commendation of Jesus's character so important here is that it comes from a first-century contemporary Jewish (opposition) source. Even without the portions of the text affirming Jesus actually rose from the dead—reputed to be Christian interpolations—this text is an important witness to the life, death, and influence of Jesus.

Pliny the Younger—Pliny the Younger was a Roman author and administrator. In a letter to Emperor Trajan (ca. 112), Pliny describes the worship practices of early Christians:

> They were in the habit of meeting on a certain fixed day before it was light, when they sang in alternate verses a hymn to Christ, as to a god, and bound themselves by a solemn oath, not to do any wicked deeds, but never to commit any fraud, theft or adultery, never to falsify their word, nor deny a trust when they should be called upon to deliver it up; after which it was their custom to separate, and then reassemble to partake of food—but food of an ordinary and innocent kind.[8]

This text makes no moral charge against Christ or even his early followers. On the contrary, it implies their behavior was exemplary.

Emperor Trajan—Trajan gives the following guidelines for punishing Christians: "No search should be made for these people; when they are denounced and found guilty they must be punished; with the restriction, however, that when the party denies himself to be a Christian, and shall give proof that he is not (that is, by adoring our gods) he shall be pardoned on the ground of repentance, even though he may have formerly incurred suspicion."[9]

This is not directly about Christ but rather about his followers. What they were deemed guilty of was not a moral indictment but political and antipolytheistic charges. From a monotheistic standpoint, however, it was a moral virtue not to worship idols.

The Talmud—The most relevant text from the Talmud is:

> On the eve of the Passover Yeshu was hanged. For forty days before the execution took place, a herald went forth and cried, "He is going forth to be stoned because he has practiced sorcery and enticed Israel to apostasy. Any one who can say anything in his favour, let him come forward and plead on his behalf." But since nothing was brought forward in his favour he was hanged on the eve of the Passover![10]

Here the charges against Christ are sorcery and enticing Israel to apostasy, neither of which is a moral flaw as such. Both are religious in nature and can easily be understood in their context. Indeed, they imply Christ's claims to deity and his miraculous confirmation of them.

Lucian—This second-century Greek writer offers sarcastic critiques of Christianity. For example:

> The Christians, you know, worship a man to this day—the distinguished personage who introduced their novel rites, and was crucified on that account. . . . You see, these misguided creatures start with the general conviction that they are immortal for all time, which explains the contempt of death and voluntary self-devotion which are so common among them; and then it was impressed on them by their original lawgiver that they are all brothers, from the moment that they are converted, and deny the gods of Greece, and worship the crucified sage, and live after his laws. All this they take quite on faith, with the result that they despise all worldly goods alike, regarding them merely as common property.[11]

Actually, there is nothing here directly against Jesus's moral character. Indeed, even his disciples are commended for their conviction and self-devotion, for living by Christ's laws, and for denying worldly goods. This certainly does not represent a moral flaw on their part or that of their leader, Jesus Christ.

Mara Bar-Serapion—He was a Syrian who wrote a letter to his son Serapion sometime between the late first and early third centuries asking, "What advantage did the Jews gain from executing their wise King? It was just after that their kingdom was abolished."[12] This reference to Jesus is positive, calling him a "wise King." It also notes that God judged them for getting rid of Christ, implying that he was good and innocent.

In short, in all the extrabiblical sources we see two things: First, there are no demonstrated moral charges against his character. Second, there are many affirmations and implications that he was morally exemplary.

The Testimony of Christ Himself

The only authentic, contemporary sources we have to what Jesus said and did are the twenty-seven books of the New Testament—especially the four Gospels. These are unanimous as to his impeccable character, which is manifest in several ways. Also, there is no firsthand witness to the contrary in existence.

Jesus Taught and Lived the Highest Ethic of the Sermon on the Mount (Matthew 5–7)

Jesus exemplifies moral perfection by proclaiming and living by the Sermon on the Mount. Even Mahatma Gandhi, the famous Hindu, was deeply impressed with the life of Jesus and particularly his Sermon on the Mount. In it and elsewhere Jesus articulates many of the great moral principles known to humankind.

The Golden Rule—Jesus says, "Whatever you want men to do to you, do also to them" (Matt. 7:12 NKJV). He views this as a summary of the

Ten Commandments, which he also affirms, as he does the entire Old Testament (Matt. 5:17). Even outside of Christianity, the Golden Rule is a widely recognized moral principle. As mentioned earlier, Confucianism has a negative form of it: "Neither do to others what you would not like them to do to you."[13] Judaism also accepts it, and even many non–Judeo-Christian religions recognize it in essence.[14] So there is virtual unanimity on the validity of this moral principle of Jesus.

Do Not Judge Others—Jesus says, "Judge not, that you be not judged. For with what judgment you judge, you will be judged" (Matt. 7:1–2 NKJV). Although it is not always understood in its original context, surveys show that this is now the most widely known verse in America. One thing is universal: few people want to be judged by others, particularly if the judgment is not fair. Jesus is not saying that we should never judge the beliefs and actions of others. Nor is he promoting the new tolerance that affirms that all ideas and beliefs are equally valid and true and no one should criticize another person's beliefs. Jesus does judge actions and beliefs of others (e.g., Matt. 6:5, 16; 11:20–24), but here he is saying that we should not judge falsely or hypocritically (Matt. 7:3–5).

Love Your Enemies—Although Jesus derives this principle from the Old Testament, many Jews of his day (Matt. 5:43–47), along with many Muslims and others, clearly are not practicing this valuable moral principle. In contrast, the Qur'an exhorts Muslims, "Take not Jews and Christians for friends. They are friends of one to another. He among you who takes them for friends is (one) of them" (Sura 5:51). Indeed, the Qu'ran urges Muslims to kill non-Muslims, declaring: "Those who believe do battle for the cause of Allah; and those who disbelieve do battle for the cause of idols. So fight the minions of the devil" (Sura 4:76).

Do Not Retaliate—In his famous Sermon on the Mount, Jesus declares, "You have heard that it was said, 'An eye for an eye and a tooth for a tooth.' But I tell you not to resist an evil person. But whoever slaps you on your right cheek, turn the other to him also" (Matt. 5:38–39 NKJV). Here is an exemplary moral principle that is widely admired but rarely practiced. Nonetheless, Jesus both promulgates and practices it (cf. Isa. 50:6).

Don't Be a Hypocrite—Jesus spends a lot of time rebuking them (e.g., Matthew 23). He declares, "Hypocrite! First remove the plank from your own eye, and then you will see clearly to remove the speck from your brother's eye" (Matt. 7:5 NKJV). The fact is that virtually no one likes a hypocrite, and so most people at least give lip service to this standard set forth by Jesus.

Don't Lust or Hate in Your Heart—In this principle Jesus takes the generally understood moral principles to another level. Most persons have not murdered, but most have hated others in their heart. Not everyone has committed an act of adultery, but who is there who has not lusted? By elevating the understanding to include the intent behind even commonly understood moral laws (Matt. 5:22, 28), Jesus takes morality to a much higher level.

Be Merciful—All the Beatitudes are part of Jesus's ethic, but "blessed are the merciful" (Matt. 5:7) is a blessing on a group of people who meet a high and hard standard. As anyone who has tried knows, it is not easy to be merciful to an enemy or an undeserving person. Indeed, popular atheist Ayn Rand teaches exactly the opposite: "To help a man who has no virtues, to help him on the ground of his suffering as such, to accept his fault, his need, as a claim—is to accept the mortgage of a zero on your values."[15] Jesus rejects this merciless standard and raises the bar to its highest level when he demands that his followers be merciful.

Keep Your Word—Breaking promises is an easy thing to do, particularly when it is more convenient to do so. But Jesus is well aware that the Torah commends those "who stand by their oath even to their hurt" (Ps. 15:4 NRSV) when he says, "Let your 'Yes' be 'Yes,' and your 'No,' 'No'" (Matt. 5:37). Keeping our word, even when it hurts us, is not easy, but we all admire this trait in others and dislike it when they do not keep their word. So again, the irony in Jesus's noble ethic is that we find it both admirable and yet humanly unattainable—which is a good indication of its divine origin.

Help the Poor—Except for Ayn Rand and her atheist followers, most people believe that we have a moral obligation to help the poor. The Bible has hundreds of verses on the topic, and Jesus makes it part of his moral agenda (e.g., Matt. 6:3–4). Interestingly, both liberals and conservatives agree that we have a moral obligation to help the poor; their disagreement is over how it should be done.

Forgive Others—Forgiveness is high on Jesus's moral agenda. He even incorporates it into his model prayer: "Forgive us our [moral] debts, as we also forgive our debtors" (Matt. 6:12). Indeed, Christ's Spirit-directed followers (John 14:26; 16:13) teach: "Even as Christ forgave you, so you also must do" (Col. 3:13 NKJV). Jesus certainly lives this in the highest degree possible when he forgives his enemies as they crucify him: "Father, forgive them; for they know not what they do" (Luke 23:34 KJV).

The Inimitable Example of Jesus

Jesus not only sets the highest moral standard, he also meets that standard. Of all the religious leaders the world has known, Jesus's life is the most inimitable.

Humility—Jesus not only teaches many marvelous moral laws, he also lives them as an example that is unmatched by anyone else who has ever lived. Though he is God in human flesh (John 1:1, 14; 1 Tim. 3:16), Jesus is a model of humility. The apostle Paul writes,

> Let this mind be in you which was also in Christ Jesus, who, being in the form of God, did not consider it robbery to be equal with God, but made Himself of no reputation, taking the form of a bondservant, and coming in the likeness of men. And being found in appearance as a man, He humbled Himself and became obedient to the point of death, even the death of the cross.
>
> Philippians 2:5–8 NKJV

No one came from higher and went lower than Jesus! His utter humility is manifest when he, the sovereign God and King of the universe, assumes the role of a servant and washes his disciples' feet (John 13:1–16).

Innocent Suffering—Jesus preached love and forgiveness even of one's enemies, but he also practiced it. Although he knows in advance who will betray him (Matt. 10:4; John 17:12), Jesus still chooses Judas as a disciple and even makes him treasurer of the group. Later when the mob comes to arrest him and Peter impetuously slices off a man's ear in an attempt to defend him, Jesus rebukes Peter and graciously heals the man's ear (Luke 22:47–51). When Jesus is falsely accused at his trial, he never speaks in his own defense (Matt. 27:12–14). As Isaiah predicts, "As a sheep before its shearers is silent, so He opened not His mouth" (Isa. 53:7 NKJV). One of Jesus's inner circle is so impressed with his innocent suffering that he writes, "For what credit is it if, when you are beaten for your faults, you take it patiently? But when you do good and suffer for it, if you take it patiently, this is commendable before God. For to this you are called, because Christ also suffered for us, leaving us an example, that you should follow His steps" (1 Peter 2:20–21 NKJV).

Dying for One's Enemies—Jesus says, "The Son of Man did not come to be served, but to serve, and to give his life as a ransom for many" (Mark 10:45), and, "I lay down my life for the sheep" (John 10:15). His disciple John declares, "God so loved the world that He gave His only begotten Son" (John 3:16 NKJV), and "He Himself is the propitiation for our sins, and not for ours only but also for the whole world. . . . For all that is in the world . . . is not of the Father but is of the world" (1 John 2:2, 16 NKJV). Paul expands on this concept: "Christ died for the ungodly. . . . Scarcely for a righteous man will one die. . . . But God demonstrated His own love toward us, in that while we were still sinners, Christ died for us" (Rom. 5:6–8 NKJV). Jesus says, "Greater love has no one than this, that he lay down his life for his friends" (John 15:13). But Jesus sacrificed his life for his enemies—a greater example of love than the world has ever seen.

Loving Little Children—Jesus is strong enough to drive out the merchants and money changers from the temple (John 2:15–16) and tough enough to rebuke religious hypocrites (Matthew 23), yet he is tender enough to be loved by little children. People even "brought little children to Him, that He might touch them." When his disciples rebuke him, he replies, "Let the little children come to Me, and do not forbid them; for of such is the kingdom of God" (Mark 10:13–14 NKJV). Indeed, he reminds adults that "unless you are converted and become as little children, you will by no means enter the kingdom of heaven" (Matt. 18:3 NKJV).

Compassion for Others—Jesus not only loves people, but he also is moved with compassion by the crowds (Matt. 9:36). As mentioned earlier, he weeps over Jerusalem, saying, "O Jerusalem, Jerusalem . . . how often I wanted to gather your children together, as a hen gathers her chicks under her wings, but you were not willing" (Matt. 23:37). Indeed, one of the most tender pictures of Jesus's heart of love is revealed at Lazarus's tomb when he weeps over the death of his beloved friend (John 11:35).

Answering Jesus's Critics

Despite the unsurpassed and unprecedented record of his righteous deeds, some have attempted to find flaws in Jesus's character. But their efforts have proved futile. Famous agnostic Bertrand Russell offered several charges against Christ.

Jesus Was Not Profoundly Humane

In his well-known book, *Why I Am Not a Christian*, agnostic Bertrand Russell argues that anyone who warns people of eternal punishment as Jesus did is not "profoundly humane."[16] The facts are not in dispute here. The Gospel record shows that Jesus repeatedly warned people about hell (Matt. 5:22, 29; 10:28; 18:9). But the conclusion Russell draws from this fact is less than convincing.

In response to the charge of being inhumane, some crucial points need to be made. To begin with, Russell's charge begs the question of whether there is a hell. He assumes there is not a hell, and hence, it is viciously inhumane to frighten people with a warning. But if there is a hell—and Jesus as the Son of God should know—then it would be profoundly inhumane *not* to warn people that they are headed there! After all, if a person sees a fire in a building and does not warn the other residents, then that individual is very inhumane. So how much greater is the need to warn others about an eternal fire to which the unrepentant are headed. Further, being a nontheist who does not believe in a moral lawgiver, one can ask where Russell got his objective moral law by which he chastises Jesus. An objective moral law implies an objective moral lawgiver, which Russell does not acknowledge.

Jesus Was Vindictive toward the Jewish Leaders

Russell also charges that Jesus reveals an angry and vindictive spirit. For example, he declares, "Woe to you blind guides. . . . Fools and blind. . . . Woe to you scribes and Pharisees, hypocrites. . . . For you are like whitewashed tombs which indeed appear beautiful outwardly, but inside are full of dead men's bones" (Matt. 23:16–17, 23, 27 NKJV). But anger against sin is not a sin; it is an act of righteousness. After all, they were not only following a path to self-destruction, but they were also taking others with them. Jesus says, "But woe to you, scribes and Pharisees, hypocrites! For you shut up the kingdom of heaven against men; for you neither go in yourselves, nor do you allow those who are entering to go in" (Matt. 23:13 NKJV). So the answer to Russell's charge is that when the Pharisees and money changers act in a manner contrary to the things of God, Christ responds with holy zeal. The purpose of his zealousness is to combat the false expressions of God[17] rather than to be vindictive.

Jesus Was Unkind

Russell also argues that anyone who unnecessarily drowns pigs is unkind, referring to Jesus driving swine into the sea, where they perished (Matt. 8:32). This argument has particular appeal in an animal-loving culture in which people are sent to prison for cruelty to animals.

In response, it should first be noted that Jesus does not drown the pigs, the demons do. Jesus casts the demons out of two men, and the demons move into the pigs. The consequent action of the demons drowning the pigs is permitted by Christ but not produced by him. There is a significant difference between permitting a potentially harmful situation—which parents do every time they allow their teens to use the family car—and promoting an accident, which good parents would never do.

Jesus is Master of his creation. As such, he can give and can take life as he wills (Deut. 32:29; Job 1:21). Indeed, he has ordained that every animal will die, and sooner or later they do. As Jesus is shown to be sovereign over inanimate creation (the sea) in the preceding story (Matt. 8:23–27), even so here he is Master of animate creatures. It is worth mentioning that unholy animals such as pigs had no place in the Holy Land; they were brought in by the Romans. And here Jesus appropriately allows the unclean spirits to go into the unclean beasts.

Finally, Russell is more concerned about the pigs than the people whom Jesus delivered from the demons. On the contrary, Jesus is more concerned about the people than the pigs. And it may have been, as *Ellicott's Commentary* points out, that "only in some such way [as allowing the demons to destroy the pigs] could the man be delivered from the inextricable confusion between himself and the unclean spirits in which he had been involved. Not till he saw the demonic forces that had oppressed him transferred to the bodies of other creatures . . . could he believe in his own deliverance."[18]

So rather than demean Christ's character, this incident confirms what is shown throughout the Gospels, namely, his compassion for persons who are in bondage to evil forces. If it is necessary to permit the sacrifice of some animals to accomplish the salvation of some humans, Jesus's compassion demonstrates that he does not hesitate to act in love for those made in God's likeness (Gen. 1:27). If we are willing to sacrifice animals for physical and temporal goods, such as food and clothes, then why should not their Creator use them for our eternal good?

In summation, the character of Christ has been well attested by both friend and foe.[19] Indeed, even Russell acknowledges elsewhere that even though Christ is not perfect (based on Russell's imperfect arguments above), nonetheless, "I grant Him a very high degree of moral goodness."[20] He also says that what the world needs is "love, Christian love, or compassion,"[21] which is a great compliment to the character of Christ. Indeed, no one has expressed any greater love than Christ (John 15:13; Rom. 5:6–8). So in spite of Russell's brilliance, a careful analysis reveals that the flaws are not in Christ's character but in Russell's arguments.

The Apologetic Implications of Christ's Sinless Character

The apologetic implications of Jesus's sinless life are obvious. No other human has ever accomplished this; even the most holy mortals have faults. His sinless character puts Christ in a class by himself and confirms his claim to be God.

In a Class by Himself

Of the great religious leaders, none even claimed to be sinless. Muhammad prayed for forgiveness (Sura 47:19); Buddha deserted his family and never returned; Mahatma Gandhi engaged in religious wars against South Africans.[22] Indeed, the great Christian saints were all painfully aware of their sinfulness. The apostle Paul cries out, "O wretched man that I am. Who shall deliver me from this body of death?" (Rom. 7:24 NKJV). Truly, "all have sinned and fall short of the glory of God" (Rom. 3:23)—except one, and his name is Jesus! This places Christ in a unique class of one. It is an apologetic of a perfect life and in itself has value in drawing people to him.

As Horace Bushnell puts it, "If Christ was a merely natural man, then was he under all the conditions private, as regards the security of his virtue, that we have discovered in man. . . . We can believe any miracle, therefore, more easily than that Christ was a man, and yet a perfect character, such as here is given." And he adds another apologetic twist: "Being a miracle himself, it would be the greatest miracle of all miracles if he did not work miracles."[23]

Confirmation of His Claim to Be God

There are other hints in the Gospels of how an impeccable life confirms the claims of Christ to be God. He himself uses the connection between virtue and truth. When those opposed to Christ reject the miracles he performs and his claim to deity, Jesus says, "Which of you convicts Me of sin?" (John 8:46 NKJV). When some of the Jewish leaders reject even Jesus's miracle of giving sight to a man born blind, others oppose them, saying, "How can a man who is a sinner do such signs?" (John 9:16 NKJV).

The connection between virtue and truth is frequently used in legal proceedings. Witnesses are discredited if they are caught in a lie. On the other hand, persons of integrity prove to be good witnesses. Jesus is unquestionably a person of integrity. Even unbelievers are "astonished at His teaching, for He taught them as one having authority, and not as the scribes" (Matt. 7:29 NKJV). Jesus could not have spoken with authority if his life cried out against what he said. As noted before, even Jesus's enemies say, "Teacher, . . . we know you are a man of integrity and that you teach the way of God in accordance with truth. You aren't swayed by men, because you pay no attention to who they are" (Matt. 22:16). With a testimony of virtue like this, it was hard to resist the conclusion that Jesus's claims to truth should be accepted.

Conclusion

Jesus not only had an apologetic, he was an apologetic. He not only persuaded people with his arguments (see chaps. 1–8), he also persuaded them with his life. Indeed, Jesus's life of sacrificial love was his greatest apology for the Christian faith.

There is something about an act of sacrificial love that persuades people of its genuineness. Mitsuo Fuchida was the Japanese pilot who led the famous air attack on Pearl Harbor. Later he became a believer because some American soldiers went to Japan after the war with the message of Jesus's love. When the Japanese pilot read for the first time the story about Jesus crying out to his Father for forgiveness of those who were crucifying him, Fuchida believed that Jesus must be the Son of God because no human being could forgive his enemies like that. He spent the rest of his life telling others about the love of Jesus.[24]

Without a doubt, love is a great apologetic. Jesus says, "By this all men will know that you are my disciples, if you love one another" (John 13:35). Love and truth are the two great weapons in the battle for the souls of men and women. Love attracts them, and truth enlightens them. Jesus says, "You will know the truth, and the truth will set you free" (John 8:32). And Paul reminds us that we should always be "speaking the truth in love" (Eph. 4:15). The wedding of the two makes a powerful apologetic.

Perhaps the most penetrating analysis of the incomparable character of Christ was penned by Horace Bushnell over a hundred years ago in his classic work, *The Character of Christ*:

> Now, one of two things must be true. He [Christ] was either sinless, or he was not. If sinless, what greater, more palpable exception to the law of human development, than that a perfect and stainless being has for once lived in the flesh! If not, . . . then we have a man taking up a religion without repentance, a religion not human, but celestial, a style of piety never taught him in his childhood, and never conceived or attempted among men; more than this, a style of piety, withal, wholly unsuited to his real character as a sinner. . . . Could there be a wider deviation from all we know of mere human development?[25]

11

Jesus and the Role of the Holy Spirit in Apologetics

While Jesus was the greatest apologist of all time (see chaps. 1–10), he nonetheless affirmed that no person can be brought to God without the ministry of the Holy Spirit. Even though he used reason and stressed evidence, yet he was well aware of the fact that neither reason nor experience alone was sufficient to elicit faith. When Peter confesses him as "the Son of the living God," Jesus responds, "Flesh and blood has not revealed this to you" (Matt. 16:17 NKJV). He knew that evidence alone, no matter how strong, is not sufficient to convince a person to believe in Christ; that is a work of God. Jesus affirmed that only the Holy Spirit can convince people of sin (John 16:8) and convert them (John 3:3–7, 14–18).

The Role of the Holy Spirit in Bringing People to Christ

Each member of the Triune God plays an important role in salvation. God the Father planned salvation, God the Son procured it, and God the Holy Spirit persuades us of its truth. Jesus was clear about the role of the Holy Spirit in enlightening people and revealing God's truth to them, as were his disciples after him. Three important roles of the Holy Spirit stand out in this context.

Convicting Us of Our Need of a Savior

None can accept Christ as Savior from sin unless they are first convinced they are sinners. And none can be convinced of sin unless the Holy Spirit convicts them. Jesus says clearly that "when He [the Holy Spirit] has come, He will convict the world of sin" (John 16:8 NKJV). Without this crucial role of the Holy Spirit, no one would ever come to Christ.

Convincing Us to Accept the Savior

Further, no one is ever convinced of the truth of Christianity apart from the ministry of the Holy Spirit. He not only convinces believers that they are sons of God (Rom. 8:16), but the Spirit alone convinces unbelievers of the truth of God. Jesus's disciple John writes, "If we receive the witness of men, the witness of God is greater" (1 John 5:9 NKJV). Jesus says, "No one can come to me unless the Father who sent me draws him" (John 6:44), and it is the Holy Spirit who strives with men and women to bring them to God (Gen. 6:3).

Converting Us to the Savior

Jesus says no one can be saved unless he is born of the Spirit, for "that which is born of the flesh is flesh, and that which is born of the Spirit is spirit" (John 3:6 NKJV). The apostle Paul identifies the Holy Spirit as the agent of regeneration whereby we move from spiritual death to spiritual life. For "you He made alive, who were dead in trespasses and sins" (Eph. 2:1 NKJV). Indeed, the Spirit not only saves but also seals believers for the day of their ultimate salvation (Eph. 4:30). No one has ever come to Christ apart from the work of the Holy Spirit; as Jesus says, "Without Me you can do nothing" (John 15:5 NKJV). And without the work of the Holy Spirit, we can do nothing to save ourselves. If this is so, what does this mean for apologetics?

The Holy Spirit Reveals the Truth about Christ

Jesus confirms that the Old Testament came by the inspiration of the Spirit of God. Citing Psalm 110:1 Jesus asks,

> How is it then that David, speaking by the Spirit, calls him [the Messiah] "Lord"? For he says,
> > "The Lord said to my Lord:
> > > 'Sit at my right hand
> > > until I put your enemies
> > > under your feet.'"

Matthew 22:43–44

David says of himself, "The Spirit of the LORD spoke through me; his word was on my tongue" (2 Sam. 23:2). By this he describes how God is the source of prophetic writing in the Old Testament, when Spirit-moved writers uttered God-breathed writings (2 Peter 1:20–21; 2 Tim. 3:16). This is why Jesus calls the Old Testament the imperishable and infallible Word of God (Matt. 5:17–18; John 10:34–35).

What Jesus confirms about the Old Testament he also promises for the New Testament. He informs his apostles that "the Helper, the Holy Spirit . . . will teach you all things, and bring to your remembrance all things that I said to you" (John 14:26 NKJV), and "when he, the Spirit of truth, comes, he will guide you into all truth" (John 16:13). So, the Holy Spirit is both the revealer and teacher of all God's truth for his followers. Indeed, Jesus's followers claimed this promise when they produced the New Testament (see 1 Cor. 14:37; Gal. 1:1; 2 Peter 3:15–16).

The Holy Spirit Teaches the Truth about Christ

Not only does the Spirit of God reveal the truth of God to the people of God, but he also teaches God's truth. As noted above, Jesus says, "The Helper, the Holy Spirit . . . *will teach you* all things" (John 14:26 NKJV, emphasis added). That his disciples understand this is evident in the writings of his beloved disciple, John:

> You have an anointing from the Holy One, and you know all things. . . . The anointing which you have received from Him abides in you, and you do not need that anyone teach you; but as the same anointing teaches you concerning all things, and is true.
>
> 1 John 2:20, 27 NKJV

No spiritual truth is ever understood unless it is taught by the Holy Spirit. This is not to say that God does not use human instruments to convey truth; he does. Indeed, the early church "continued steadfastly in the apostles' doctrine" (Acts 2:42 KJV). The end result is that through whatever or whomever one learns a truth about Christ, it is God the Holy Spirit who is the effective cause of that truth.

The Relationship between the Holy Spirit and Apologetic Evidence

While granting the necessity of the Holy Spirit in convincing and converting people to Christ, Jesus saw no contradiction between a strong rational and evidential apologetic and the active role of the Holy Spirit (see chaps. 1–10). There are important reasons for this.

First, while evidence that Christ is the Son of God is a necessary condition for salvation, nonetheless, it is not a sufficient condition. No one ever believes in God without first having evidence that God exists, for "since the creation of the world His invisible attributes are clearly seen, being understood by the things that are made, even His eternal power and Godhead, so that they are without excuse" (Rom. 1:20 NKJV). There is always evidence that is "clearly seen" in general revelation before a person believes in God. Hebrews declares that "anyone who comes to him [God] must believe that he exists" (Heb. 11:6). So, everyone who believes in the true God (or the true Christ) first has some kind of evidence that he exists—even though it may be small.

Paul says to the heathen at Lystra that God "has not left himself without testimony: He has shown kindness by giving you rain from heaven and crops in their seasons; he provides you with plenty of food and fills your hearts with joy" (Acts 14:17). Likewise, no one ever places his faith in the true Christ (who was a first-century historical figure) without some kind of evidence that he existed, even if it is only the internal evidence in the Gospel record or the external testimony of someone who is deemed a reliable source and has viewed the evidence.

In brief, even though evidence is insufficient in itself to draw an unbeliever to Christ, nevertheless, it is a necessary step in that process. Only the Holy Spirit can bring a person to Christ, but he uses evidence as a means by which he convinces an individual of the need to accept Christ.

Evidence Can Be an Instrumental Cause of Salvation

Even if evidence were not a necessary precondition for saving faith, it would not be incompatible with God's ways to use it as a means for reaching people for Christ. Granted, Jesus taught that the Holy Spirit alone is the efficient cause of our salvation, but it does not follow that evidence cannot be an instrumental cause of salvation. That is to say, while evidence itself does not bring about anyone's salvation, it can be a means through which the efficient work of the Holy Spirit produces salvation in a person's life.

It would be insulting to the revealed nature of God the Holy Spirit to say that he—the all-knowing, all-wise, and most rational being in the universe—would bypass reason to reach rational creatures made in his image (Gen. 1:27). In fact, it is unreasonable to disjoin a rational God from a rational process by which he wishes to reach his rational offspring (see Acts 17:29).

God is sovereign and can utilize any noncontradictory means he wishes to save repentant creatures. God sometimes uses his goodness to lead people to repentance (Rom. 2:4), and he sometimes uses tragedy to accomplish his purposes (Gen. 50:20). So if he desires to use apologetic evidence as part of that process, then who can deny him of the opportunity?

And if answers to an honest seeker's questions will help him or her toward Christ, there is every reason to believe that God will give that person all the reasons he or she realistically needs to make a reasonable decision to become a believer. Of course, Jesus never cast "pearls before swine" (Matt. 7:6) who were really not sincere, and he did not perform a miracle to satisfy anyone's curiosity (Luke 23:8). But he did provide ample evidence for any honest seeker— many of whom have become believers and have testified to this over the centuries. Indeed, many famous believers came to Christ through this route, including Simon Greenleaf, Frank Morrison, and C. S. Lewis.[1]

The Distinction between Proof and Persuasion

The word *proof* speaks of objective certainty; the word *persuasion* refers to subjective certitude. Proof can be provided by reason and evidence, albeit in terms of degrees of probability ranging from *absolute certainty* at the top, through *moral certainty, high probability of it being beyond all doubt*, and *beyond all reasonable doubt* at the bottom. Apologetics deals with objective truth, but as such it cannot provide subjective certitude about the truths of the Christian faith. That comes only from the witness of the Holy Spirit in and through that evidence. This distinction has been manifest in various ways in the works of great Christian thinkers down through the ages.

In spite of the supernatural proof Jesus provided for his claims, many were not persuaded. John writes, "Even after Jesus had done all these miraculous signs in their presence, they still would not believe in him" (John 12:37). Indeed, Jesus says of the hard-hearted, "They will not be convinced even if someone rises from the dead" (Luke 16:31). Luke tells of many infallible proofs Jesus presented for his resurrection, yet not everyone believed. Sheer objective proof alone is insufficient to produce belief in spiritual matters; one must also be persuaded by the Holy Spirit. And even then, the will can "resist the Holy Spirit" (Acts 7:51).

Faith of Our Fathers

Many of the great Christian fathers and later teachers in the Christian church have articulated a view similar to that of Jesus. A few citations will support the point about the view of Jesus on the relation between apologetics and the role of the Holy Spirit.

St. Augustine (354–430)

St. Augustine puts it: "No one indeed believes anything unless he has first thought that it is to be believed." Hence, "It is necessary that everything which is believed should be believed after thought has led the way."[2] He adds elsewhere, "God forbid that He should hate in us that faculty [of reason] by which He made us superior to all other beings. Therefore, we must refuse so to believe as not to receive or seek reason for our belief, since we could not believe at all if we did not have rational souls."[3] Only when one does believe, however, is that person instructed by the Holy Spirit in the things of God. For "we believe that we might know."[4] "First believe, then understand."[5] "It is sin which deceives the soul,"[6] therefore only by the work of the Holy Spirit can we by faith receive the truths of God. "Faith, therefore, avails to the knowledge and to the love of God,"[7] and this faith is confirmed by supernatural acts of God, for "miracles were necessary before the world believed, in order that it might believe."[8]

Thomas Aquinas (1224–1274)

Aquinas believes that "in Sacred Teaching we can use philosophy in a threefold way." First, "we can use it to demonstrate the preambles of faith . . . for example, that God exists, that God is one, or similar propositions concerning God or creatures that faith proposes as having been proved in philosophy."[9] He argues that "human reasoning in support of what we believe may stand in a two-fold relation to the will of the believer. First, as preceding the act of the will, as, for instance, when a man either has not the will, or not a prompt will, to believe, unless he be moved by human reason; and in this way human reasoning diminishes the merit of faith." For "he ought to believe matters of faith, not because of human reasoning, but because of the divine authority." Second, "human reasons may be consequent to the will of the believer." For "when a man has a will ready to believe, he loves the truth he believes, he thinks out and takes to heart whatever reasons he can find in support thereof; and in this way, human reasoning does not exclude the merit of faith, but is a sign of greater merit."[10]

Aquinas propounds that faith is supported by, though not based on, probable evidence. "Those who place their faith in this truth, however, 'for which the human reason offers no experimental evidence,' do not believe foolishly, as though 'following artificial fables.' " Rather, faith "reveals its own presence, as well as the truth of its teaching and inspiration, by fitting arguments; and in order to confirm those truths that exceed natural knowledge, it gives visible manifestations to works that surpass the ability of all nature."[11]

True faith, in Aquinas's view, results from the work of the Holy Spirit. Reason may accompany faith but it does not cause faith. "Faith is called a consent without inquiry in so far as the consent of faith, or assent, is not caused by an investigation of the understanding." Commenting on Ephesians 2:8–9, Aquinas contends that faith is produced by God: "Free will is inadequate for the act of faith since the contents of faith are above reason. . . . That a man should believe, therefore, cannot occur from himself unless God gives it."[12]

Of course, Aquinas believed that an act of free will, prompted by God's grace, was necessary to receive God's gift. So reasoning "can accompany the assent of faith" but it never causes it. That is because "faith involves will (freedom) and reason doesn't coerce the will."[13] In other words, a person is free to dissent even though there may be convincing reasons to believe.

One can know that God exists by reason, but in order to believe *in* God, one must have the inner testimony of the Holy Spirit. "One who believes does have a sufficient motive for believing, namely the authority of God's teaching, confirmed by miracles, and—what is greater—the inner inspiration [*instinctus*] of God inviting him to believe."[14] This consent to believe, however, is not coerced, for there are two kinds of causes that bring a person to belief: "One is a cause that persuades from without, for example, a miracle witnessed or a human appeal urging belief." Second, "No such cause is enough, however; one man believes and another does not, when both have seen the same miracle, heard the same preaching. Another kind of cause must therefore be present, an inner cause; one that influences a person inwardly to assent to the things of faith." Hence, "The assent of faith, which is its principal act, therefore, has as its cause God, moving us inwardly through grace." This "belief is, of course, a matter of the believer's will, but a person's will needs to be prepared by God through his grace in order to be lifted up to what surpasses nature."[15]

How can we be sure when the support of our faith rests on many intermediary (fallible) testimonies? Aquinas responds, "All the intermediaries through which faith comes to us are above suspicion. We believe the prophets and apostles because the Lord has been their witness by performing miracles, as Mark says" [16:20]. Furthermore, "We believe the successors of the apostles and prophets only in so far as they tell us those things which the apostles and prophets have left in their writings."[16] The Bible alone, inspired by the Holy Spirit, is the final and infallible authority for our faith.

Contrary to a widely held misconception, Aquinas did not believe that reason in itself can provide the basis for believing in God. It can only prove *that* God exists, but it cannot convince an unbeliever to believe *in* God, for "they do not truly believe in God."[17] We may believe (assent without reservation) in something that is neither self-evident nor deduced from the self-evident (where the intellect is moved) by a movement of the will.

This does not mean, however, that reason plays no prior role to belief, for "he would not believe unless he saw that they are worthy of belief on the basis of evident signs or something of the sort."[18] In other words, "Faith does not involve a search by natural reason to prove what is believed. But it does involve a form of enquiry unto things by which a person is led to belief, e.g. whether they are spoken by God and confirmed by miracles."[19]

Demons, for example, are convinced by the evidence that God exists, but it "is not their wills which bring demons to assent to what they are said to believe. Rather, they are forced by the evidence of signs which convince them that what the faithful believe is true." But "these signs do not cause the appearance of what is believed so that the demons could on this account be said to see those things which are believed. Therefore, belief is predicated equivocally of men who believe and of demons."[20]

John Calvin (1509–1564)

John Calvin's position is widely misunderstood, even by some of his most ardent followers. It is actually very much like that of Thomas Aquinas.[21] Calvin held that there were objective proofs for God's existence, speaking of "the invisible and incomprehensible essence of God, to a certain extent, made visible in his works" and of "proofs of the soul's immortality." For "on each of his [God's] works his glory is engraven in characters so bright, so distinct, and so illustrious, that none, however dull and illiterate, can plead ignorance as their excuse."[22] Commenting on Romans 1:20–21, Calvin concludes that Paul "plainly testifies here, that God has presented to the minds of all the means of knowing him, having so manifested himself by his works, that they must necessarily see what of themselves they seek not to know—that there is some God." In the light of the evidence, even unbelievers "will be compelled to confess that the Scripture exhibits clear evidence of its being spoken by God, and, consequently, of its containing his heavenly doctrine."[23]

So even though the use of human reason is not absolute, yet it does bring a sufficient conviction about both the existence of God and the truth of Scripture. Calvin says, "We receive it [Scripture] reverently, and according to its dignity, those proofs which were not so strong as to produce and rivet a full conviction in our minds, become most appropriate helps." Calvin speaks of "the credibility of Scripture sufficiently proved, in so far as natural reason admits."[24] He even offers rational "proofs"[25] from various areas, including: the dignity, truth, simplicity, and efficacy of Scripture. To this he adds evidence from miracles, prophecy, church history, and the martyrs.[26]

Calvin also believed, however, that no one ever came to be convinced of the certainty of truths about God, Christ, and the Bible apart from the supernatural work of the Holy Spirit. He saw no contradiction between this and what he said about the natural knowledge of God in all people, even about many of these same truths. Calvin believed that the depravity of the human will obscures a person's ability to understand and respond to this natural revelation of God. He writes, "Your idea of his [God's] nature is not clear unless you acknowledge him to be the origin and foundation of all goodness. Hence, would arise both confidence in him and a desire of cleaving to him, did not the depravity of the human mind lead it away from the proper course of investigation."[27] In order to overcome this problem, it is necessary for the Holy Spirit to bring greater certainty. Calvin says, "Our faith in doctrine is not established until we have a perfect conviction that God is its author. Hence, the highest proof of Scripture is uniformly taken from the character of him whose word it is." So "our conviction of the truth of Scripture must be derived from a higher source than human conjecture, judgments, or reasons; namely, the secret testimony of the Spirit."[28]

Using reason to defend Scripture is insufficient. As Calvin puts it, "Although we may maintain the sacred Word of God against gainsayers, it does not follow that we shall forthwith implant the certainty which faith requires in their hearts." Calvin insists that "the testimony of the Spirit is superior to reason. For as God alone can properly bear witness to his own words, so these words will not obtain full credit in the hearts of men, until they are sealed by the inward testimony of the Spirit." He adds, "The same Spirit, therefore, who spoke by the mouth of the prophets, must penetrate our hearts, in order to convince us that they faithfully delivered the message with which they were divinely entrusted."[29]

"Let it therefore be held as fixed, that those who are inwardly taught by the Holy Spirit acquiesce implicitly in Scripture; that Scripture, carrying its own evidence along with it, deigns not to submit to proofs and arguments, but owes the full conviction with which we ought to receive it to the testimony of the Spirit." Thus, "Enlightened by him, we no longer believe, either on our own judgment or that of others, that the Scriptures are from God; but, in a way superior to human judgment, feel perfectly assured . . . that it came to us, by the instrumentality of men, from the very mouth of God."[30]

So "we ask not for proofs or probabilities on which to rest our judgment, but we subject our intellect and judgment to it as too transcendent for us to estimate." The assurance the Spirit gives "is a conviction which asks not for reasons; such, a knowledge which accords with the highest reason, namely, the knowledge in which the mind rests more firmly and securely than in any reason; such, in fine, the conviction which revelation from heaven alone can produce."[31] Thus, "In vain were the authority of Scripture fortified by argument, or supported by the consent of the Church, or confirmed by any other helps, if unaccompanied by an assurance higher and stronger than human judgment can give. Till this better foundation had been laid, the authority of Scripture remains in suspense."[32]

This proper understanding of Calvin was carried on by Francis Turretin (seventeenth century), B. B. Warfield (1851–1921), Kenneth Kantzer (1917–2002), John Gerstner (1914–1996), and R. C. Sproul (b. 1939). The latter sees the issue clearly when he declares that "the testimonium is not placed over against reason as a form of mysticism or subjectivism. Rather, it goes beyond and transcends reason."[33] In short, it is God working through objective evidence, not apart from it, that provides us with subjective certainty that the Bible is the Word of God; it is a combination of the objective and subjective, not an exclusion of the objective evidence by a subjective experience.

Likewise, B. B. Warfield believed that the indicia (indications of the Bible's divine character) are side-by-side cofactors with the Holy Spirit to convince people of the truth of the Bible. Warfield agreed with Calvin that the indicia are not in themselves capable of bringing people to Christ or even convincing them of the complete, divine authority of Scripture. Nonetheless, Warfield held that the Holy Spirit always exercises his convincing power through them. He writes, "It is easy, of course, to say that a Christian man must take his standpoint not above the Scriptures, but in the Scriptures. He very certainly must. But surely he must first have Scriptures, authenticated to him as such, before he can take his standpoint in them."[34] To do this, "the world of facts is open to all people and all can be convinced of God's existence and the truth of Scripture through them by the power of reasoning of a redeemed thinker."

In his 1908 article "Apologetics," Warfield says, "Though faith be a moral act and a gift of God, it is yet formally conviction passing into confidence; and . . . all forms of conviction must rest on evidence as their ground, and it is not faith but reason which investigates the nature and validity of this ground." So "we believe in Christ because it is rational to believe in Him, not even though it be irrational."[35]

Of course, Warfield believes, like Calvin, that "mere reasoning cannot make a Christian; but that is not because faith is not the result of evidence, but because a dead soul cannot respond to evidence. . . . The action of the Holy Spirit in giving faith is not apart from evidence, but along with evidence; and in the first instance consists in preparing the soul for the reception of the evidence." Warfield adds that "this is not to argue that it is by apologetics that men are made Christians, but that apologetics supplies to Christian men the systematically organized basis on which the faith of Christian men must rest."[36]

The relationship, then, between reason and evidence on the one side and the Holy Spirit on the other is complimentary. It is not either the Holy Spirit or evidence; it is the Holy Spirit working in and through evidence to convince people of the truth of Christianity. There is both an outer (objective) dimension and an inner (subjective) dimension to the process by which people come to know Christianity is true. But what is important is that the two domains are never separated, as many Christian mystics and inner-light subjectivists claim.[37]

Jonathan Edwards (1703–1758)

According to the great Puritan thinker Jonathan Edwards, reason has many functions. It can "prove the existence of God, the Revealer. . . . Reason anticipates that there will be a revelation. . . . Reason alone can grasp rationally any 'pretended' revelation. . . . Reason must verify any revelation as genuine. . . . Reason argues revelation's dependability. . . . Reason, having anticipated mysteries in any genuine divine revelation, defends them, refuting any objections to their presence. . . . Though the 'divine and supernatural light' does not come from reason, it is reason that comprehends what this light illuminates."[38]

Contrary to Calvin, Edwards held that reason not only can prove God's existence, but it can do this with certainty. For it is impossible that nothing could cause something. And since something now exists, reasoned Edwards, it follows necessarily that there must be an eternal and necessary being (i.e., God). Edwards's firm conviction about this springs from the law of causality, which he describes as a self-evident principle, a "dictate of common sense," "the mind of mankind," and "this grand principle of common sense."[39] In "Miscellanies" he declares that "'Tis acknowledged by all to be self-evident that nothing can begin without a cause." Thus, "when understood 'tis a truth that irresistibly will have place in the assent." This being the case, "if we suppose a time wherein there was nothing, a body will not of its own accord begin to be." For to hold that something can arise without a cause is "what the understanding abhors."[40]

Edwards was just as certain that human reason demonstrates that God must have certain attributes. He asserts, "It is evident, by Scripture and reason, that God is infinitely, eternally, unchangeably, and independently glorious and happy,"[41] for that which is necessary and independent must be infinite.

This does not mean that there was no role for the Holy Spirit in Edwards's apologetic. He enumerates four limitations to human reason: "First, it cannot make the knowledge of God 'real' to unregenerate man. Second, it cannot yield a supernatural, salvific revelation or even 'sense' it by mere reason. Third, if it does receive a revelation, it cannot thereafter determine what that revelation may and may not contain. Fourth, it cannot even 'apprehend' divine revelation as divine revelation, though it may recognize its presence."[42]

This does not eliminate the need for supernatural revelation by the Holy Spirit. As Edwards says, "Were it not for divine revelation, I am persuaded that there is no one doctrine of that which we call natural religion, which, notwithstanding all philosophy and learning, would not be forever involved in darkness, doubts, endless disputes, and dreadful confusion." In fact, "the philosophers had the foundation of most of their truths, from the ancients, or from the Phoenicians, or what they picked up here and there of the relics of revelation."[43]

Even though it is possible for natural reason to construct valid arguments for the existence of God, Edwards denies that any non-Christian thinkers ever did this. He asks "whether nature and reason alone can give us a right idea of God, and are sufficient to establish among mankind a clear and sure knowledge of his nature, and the relation we stand in to him, and his concerns with us?" His answer is emphatic: "There never was a man known or heard of, who had an [right] idea of God, without being taught it." This is why "the increase of learning and philosophy in the Christian world, is owing to revelation. The doctrines of revealed religion are the foundation of all useful and excellent knowledge." Thus, "the Word of God leads barbarous nations into the way of using their understandings. It brings their minds into a way of reflecting and abstracted reasoning; and delivers from uncertainty in the first principles, such as, the being of God, the dependence of all things upon him. . . . Such principles as these are the basis of all true philosophy, as appears more and more as philosophy improves."[44]

Edwards holds that "it is one thing, to work out a demonstration of a point, when once it is proposed: and another, to strike upon the point itself. I cannot tell whether any man would have considered the works of creation as effects, if he had never been told they had a cause." Indeed, "the best reasoner in the world, endeavoring to find out the causes of things, by the things themselves, might be led into the grossest errors and contradictions, and find himself, at the end, in extreme want of an instructor."[45] In whatever we know about this true God from revelations, it is possible to construct a valid argument for his existence on the basis of premises drawn from nature and reason alone. So special revelation is not in principle logically necessary to prove the existence of the true God, but it was in practice historically necessary to have special revelation before this is accomplished. "Whether we consider what the human understanding could do, or what it actually did," Edwards says plainly, "it could not have attained to a sufficient knowledge of God without revelation."[46]

Notwithstanding all of his stress on rational and objective evidence, Edwards did not believe that either general or special revelations were sufficient to make depraved men and women open to God's truth. In addition to objective special revelation, there had to be a subjective, divine illumination. Only "the divine and supernatural light" could open a person's heart to receive God's revelation. Without this divine illumination, no one ever comes to accept God's revelation, regardless of how strong the evidence for it is. A new heart is needed, not a new brain. This is accomplished by the illumination of the Holy Spirit. This divine light does not give any new truth or new revelations. Rather, it provides a new heart, a new attitude of receptivity by which one is able to accept God's truth.[47]

Summary of the Great Apologists on the Role of the Holy Spirit in Apologetics

In summary, most classical apologetics agree on the following roles of the Holy Spirit in reference to apologetics:

1. The Holy Spirit plays a necessary role in the origin of a revelation that is superior to general revelation in nature, namely, a special revelation in Scripture.
2. The Holy Spirit is needed for understanding the spiritual implications of revealed truth.
3. The Holy Spirit is necessary for full assurance of the truths of Christianity.
4. The Holy Spirit alone prompts individuals to believe in God's saving truth.
5. The Holy Spirit works in and through evidence but not separate from it.
6. As the Spirit of a rational God, he never bypasses the head (reason) in order to reach the heart.
7. The Spirit of God provides supernatural evidence (miracles) in confirmation of Christianity.

Now it seems to us that this view is more faithful to that of the one held by Jesus than the other major apologetic positions (see chap. 12).

Conclusion

It is granted that none are saved apart from the gracious work of the Holy Spirit in convicting them of sin and converting them to the Savior. It is also true that this same Spirit, a member of the omniscient (all-knowing) Godhead, knows that reason is a helpful, if not necessary, means of bringing rational people to Christ. Indeed, the evidence (see chaps. 1–10) is that this is exactly what Jesus taught. And no one has ever demonstrated that this is contradictory to his affirmations about the necessary role of the Holy Spirit in our salvation.

Jesus saw that belief (which calls for evidence) is an important precondition for belief in Christ as the Son of God, for it is not reasonable to ask someone to believe in something for which he or she has no evidence to believe that it is true. For instance, no rational person steps into an elevator unless he or she can see a solid floor there. But all the evidence in the world that an elevator is safe and sound does not coerce anyone to get in it. That is a step of faith. But it is a step of faith in the light of the evidence rather than a leap of faith in the absence of evidence. So it is with the Christian faith and the apologetic of Jesus.

Apologetic evidence is crucial to belief that Christ is the Son of God, but the Holy Spirit is essential to belief in Christ as the Son of God. Apologetics can bring about intellectual assent, but only the Holy Spirit can change the heart.

Jesus commands, "Love the Lord your God . . . with all your mind" as well as "with all your heart" (Matt. 22:37). It is true that God desires to reach our heart and not merely our head, but it is also true that God does not wish to bypass the head on the way to the heart. So it is not either the Holy Spirit or apologetics; rather, it is the Holy Spirit working through apologetic arguments and evidence to bring people to the truth. Jesus illustrated this perfectly in his life and teachings.

12

Jesus's Apologetic Method

Jesus never set forth a formal apologetic methodology. Of course, he also never set forth a systematic treatment on any of the great doctrines of the Christian faith, yet he clearly believed in the doctrines of the divine inspiration of the Old Testament (Matt. 5:17–18; John 10:34–35), his sacrificial atonement (Mark 10:45), his physical resurrection (Matt. 12:40; John 2:18–21), the Trinity (Matt. 3:16–17; 28:18–20), his bodily ascension (John 16:5–7), and his second coming (Matthew 24–25). Jesus had no more need to set forth a systematic approach to apologetics than he did to explain a systematic approach to ethics (Matt. 22:36–40). He simply did apologetics as part of his attempt to reach and persuade people of the truth he proclaimed. In short, he had a practical apologetic, but he never stated a theoretical one. Nonetheless, there is an apologetic method implicit in what Jesus did and said. In fact, he used many different ways to reach many different people.

So did Jesus express an apologetic system? The answer is explicitly *No* but implicitly *Yes*, but one must piece it together from the various strategies he used to reach people. Just what that was will be discussed later. First, we will examine the various practical strategies Jesus used to persuade people of his message.

Jesus's Practical Apologetic Approaches

On a practical level, Jesus was a master at beginning where people were and then taking them to where he wanted them to go. Sometimes this involved interrogations, and other times it entailed affirmations. At all times it involved careful argumentation. From the preceding chapters, several elements of his practical methodology emerge.

Socratic Method

Jesus often uses the so-called Socratic method of asking questions to draw out the answer he desires from his opponents, as he does with the rich young ruler (Luke 18:18–23). In one case this method is so effective that his opponents never ask him another question. When he asks the Pharisees, who did not accept his deity, to explain why David called the Messiah "Lord" (in Ps. 110:1), "no one was able to answer Him in a word, nor from that day on did anyone dare question Him anymore" (Matt. 22:46 NKJV).

Reduction Method

Jesus is also adept at reducing an opposing view to the absurd. Matthew 12:22–28 is a good example. Here the Pharisees claim he is exorcising demons by the power of the devil. Jesus demonstrates that their premise leads to a contradiction: "Every kingdom divided against itself will be ruined, and every city or household divided against itself will not stand. If Satan drives out Satan, he is divided against himself. How then can his kingdom stand? And if I drive out demons by Beelzebub, by whom do your people drive them out?" (vv. 25–27). Since their view leads logically to an absurd conclusion, it is false.

A Fortiori Method

One of Jesus's favorite rational procedures is showing that his teachings follow with greater force than those things his audience holds to be true. When Jesus desires to heal someone on the Sabbath, which the Pharisees say is contrary to the law, Jesus asks, "If any of you has a sheep and it falls into a pit on the Sabbath, will you not take hold of it and lift it out?" Of course, they would. So Jesus continues, "How much more valuable is a man than a sheep!" The conclusion is obvious: "Therefore it is lawful to do good [and heal] on the Sabbath" (Matt. 12:11–12).

Parabolic Method

Using a story to convey a truth is called *parabolic apologetics*. The great apologist C. S. Lewis used the power of story in his Narnia series as well as in *The Great Divorce*. Most people who have read the Narnia series fall in love with Aslan, the lion who died and rose from the dead. We know a Jewish girl who had rejected Jesus as her Messiah until she read *The Last Battle* from Lewis's Narnia series. She so fell in love with Aslan that when she finally realized he represented Jesus, she overcame her cultural barriers that had kept her from accepting Jesus as her Messiah and became a Christian.

In *The Great Divorce* Lewis presents a narrative of a bus ride from hell to heaven. The people from hell feel completely out of place in heaven because the people there are eternally doing what those from hell hate—namely, submitting to God's will. As a result, they are more miserable in heaven than in hell. Through this story Lewis defends the doctrine of hell and explains why it is consistent with the nature of God and yet honors the free will of men and women who are created in the image of God.

Fyodor Dostoevsky, in his brilliant novel *The Brothers Karamazov*, presents an excellent example of the parabolic method. In his chapter titled "The Grand Inquisitor," Dostoevsky's characters wrestle with the problem of evil and the existence of God. Through their discussion Dostoevsky presents a well-reasoned argument from the atheist brother, Ivan. Alyosha's response is a powerful argument for the existence of God. He explains that if God does not exist, there really is no absolute moral standard by which we can judge an act as good or evil. If there is no God, we are reduced to moral relativism, and no act, however dreadful, can be condemned by the atheist. Since this position is unlivable, Dostoevsky, through Alyosha, exposes the failure of the atheist position.

John Bunyan, through the use of allegory, brilliantly tells the story of the Christian journey in his novel, *Pilgrim's Progress*, which remains one of the most widely read books of modern time. It has long held a position second only to the Bible in popularity. Why? Because Christian truth is powerfully expressed in parabolic form in a way that indelibly impresses itself upon the mind of the reader.

Even the stories of non-Christian authors can be used in the defense of Christianity. The writings of Jean Paul Sartre and Albert Camus reveal truth about the meaning of life from an atheist perspective. These great writers discovered and conveyed the truth that if God does not exist, life is ultimately meaningless. As the writer of Ecclesiastes states, "'Meaningless! Meaningless!' says the Teacher. 'Utterly meaningless! Everything is meaningless'" (1:2). The writings of atheists can be used to present the inevitable conclusion of naturalism and then point an atheist to the inconsistency of his or her own position.

Of course, Jesus is the master at parabolic apologetics—using a familiar story, the point of which is accepted by his audience, in order to convey his truth. His parables, with which we are so familiar, are some of the world's great short stories, and they distinguish his apologetic more than any other method he employs.

But what exactly is parabolic apologetics? Some of its characteristics may be briefly described as follows:

1. *It is apologetics expressed in story form.* Everyone loves a good story, and it is a very effective way to get a point across.

2. *It is an indirect form of apologetics.* As opposed to direct discourse, for which opponents have their defenses up, parabolic apologetics catches people with their guard down. They find themselves affirming the point before they realize that the point applies to them.

3. *It is apologetics with a hidden but powerful logic.* The logic is a kind of a fortiori. It says in effect, if I accept this as true in everyday matters of life, how much more should I accept it in spiritual and eternal matters? For example, as in the parable of the one lost sheep, I realize that the shepherd would leave the ninety-nine for a short time to find and save one lost animal. How much more is that true of one lost human for all time?

4. *Parabolic apologetic aids in self-discovery.* People are carried along with the story until they discover for themselves what the point is. And self-discovery is an important strategy for learning. It makes people feel they have found this truth for themselves, even though it is the storyteller who has guided them carefully and inevitably to this conclusion.

5. *Parabolic apologetics is also depravity sensitive.* None of us likes to be told outright that we are a sinner, a hypocrite, or the like, but we can easily see it in another person. Thus, the depravity sensitivity of parabolic apologetics is that it helps us recognize the sin or error of another person—the one in the story—before we realize it is speaking about us.

When King David hears Nathan's account of a rich man with many sheep who takes a poor man's lamb, he is indignant and pronounces judgment on the rich man (2 Sam. 12:1–6). Then Nathan the prophet says to him, "You are the man!" (v. 7). At that point it is too late for David to deny his sin, which has been exposed by Nathan's parable: he had taken Uriah's wife, Bathsheba, and then caused Uriah's death.

Conviction of sin can be painful (Psalm 51). But parabolic apologetics that is depravity sensitive uses the indirect technique of a story to get the point across. By the time the point is made, it is too late to escape the a fortiori logic.

What Jesus Did Not Believe about Apologetics

From a careful analysis of Jesus's life and teachings in the Gospels, several things emerge. Some inform us of what Jesus did not believe, and others tell us what he did believe regarding apologetics. First, let's discuss what Jesus did not believe about apologetics.

Jesus Was Not a Fideist

Jesus did not expect people to believe that what he said was true simply by faith. Instead, he offered good evidence for his claims. Jesus's call to follow him included not only powerful teaching but also a strong defense of his ministry and assertions. Apologetics was an essential part of his ministry; he used Scripture, reason, evidence, the testimony of witnesses, miracles, his resurrection, and even an appeal to people's existential needs to confirm his claims. He clearly was not a fideist.

Jesus Was Not a Pure Evidentialist

Jesus did not believe, however, that one could be saved by apologetic evidence alone. He understood the difference between *belief that*, which requires evidence, and *belief in*, which involves an act of the will. He knew evidence was the ground for belief that something is true, but he also knew that evidence alone was not sufficient to produce belief unto salvation.

Rational people need evidence to believe that something is true, and Jesus constantly provided it. But he also knew that *belief that* was not sufficient to get a person into his kingdom. The individual must make a choice—an act of the will—to believe in him (John 14:1).

Jesus knew the difference between a mere *professor* of salvation and one who truly *possesses* it. This is why he speaks so often about false prophets (Matt. 7:15; 24:24) and those who falsely profess him, saying, "Lord, Lord, did we not prophesy in your name?" (Matt. 7:22). Hence, he constantly appeals to people's will to believe in him: "Whoever believes in Him should not perish but have eternal life. . . . He who believes in the Son has everlasting life; and he who does not believe in the Son shall not see life, but the wrath of God abides on him" (John 3:15, 36 NKJV; see also 5:24).[1]

Jesus Was Not a Pure Rationalist

Although Jesus used rational arguments very effectively (see chap. 4), he was not a rationalist in the deductive sense as defined by modern philosophy (such as in Benedict Spinoza and Rene Descartes). His approach was not *a priori* (independent of experience) but *a posteriori* (beginning with experience); he appealed to people's senses as well as their reason.

After the resurrection, Jesus says to his unbelieving disciples, "Behold My hands and My feet, that it is I Myself. Handle Me and see, for a spirit does not have flesh and bones as you see I have" (Luke 24:39 NKJV). Likewise, Jesus addresses Thomas's doubts, "Reach your finger here, and look at My hands; and reach your hand here, and put it into My side. Do not be unbelieving, but believing" (John 20:27 NKJV). As John later says, "That which was from the beginning, which we have heard, which we have seen with our eyes, which we have looked upon, and our hands have handled . . . was manifested, and we have seen, and bear witness" (1 John 1:1–2 NKJV).

Jesus's Apologetic Was Not Devoid of the Spirit

As discussed at length in chapter 11, Jesus understood completely that no person can be brought to salvation without the ministry of the Holy Spirit, no matter how strong the rational and evidential apologetic. Even though he used reason and stressed evidence, he knew that neither of these were sufficient to elicit faith. Jesus affirms that only the Holy Spirit can convince people of sin and convert them when he tells Nicodemus, "I assure you, no one can enter the Kingdom of God without being born of water and the Spirit. Humans can reproduce only human life, but the Holy Spirit gives birth to spiritual life. So don't be surprised when I say, 'You must be born again'" (John 3:5–7 NLT; see also 16:7–8).

Jesus Was Not a Presuppositionalist

It is not surprising that Jesus was not a presuppositional apologist.[2] That would have entailed beginning his apologetics with the Triune God, as revealed in the Holy Scriptures, and then reasoning from there. Since the Jews were already monotheists, there was no need to convince them of what they already believed. But it is clear that Jesus would offer evidence for God to those who did not believe he exists—which is obvious from what he taught his disciples and other followers (see chap. 8). Also, Jesus did not believe that unsaved people were so blinded by sin that they could not understand the message and had to be regenerated before they could believe.[3] Instead he began his teachings with the common ground of general revelation, in everyday things the people could experience. This master teacher taught the unfamiliar in terms of the familiar, and he rebuked those who failed to use sound reason (cf. John 3:12).

Jesus Was Not a Rational Coherentist

Although Jesus believed in the law of noncontradiction as a test for false views (see chap. 4), he did not begin and end his apologetics in the thin air of rational thought. He did not believe, as some apologists do,[4] that logical coherency is the total test for the truth of a worldview, for there are many coherent beliefs that are false. For example, the statements of conspirators who lie may be coherent, but they are still false. And some opposing worldviews are coherent with their own starting points, but not all can justify these starting points. A beautiful dream can be a coherent picture, but it is not grounded in reality.

What Jesus Did Believe about Apologetics

Positively speaking, there were many things that Jesus did believe and practice that reveal his apologetic approach. Each of these contribute to an overall apologetic approach that will be named and characterized at the end.

Jesus Believed in the Use of Reason

Jesus was familiar with and utilized all the basic laws of rational thought and reasoning processes. This included the laws of identity, noncontradiction, and excluded middle. He employed categorical, hypothetical, and disjunctive syllogisms. In addition, he knew how to use a reductio ad absurdum argument and avoid the horns of a dilemma presented by an opponent. Jesus also often utilized an a fortiori argument—showing that given what his audience believed, they should accept his teaching with even greater force (see chap. 4).

Jesus Believed in the Use of Evidence

The apologetics of Jesus involved the testimony of credible witnesses. In John 5:31–46 Jesus presents the testimony of several key witnesses whose integrity and authority are unquestionably sound: John the Baptist, Moses, God the Father, the Old Testament, and his own life and miracles. He was not a fideist who asked for a blind leap of faith but rather an evidentialist who provided sufficient evidence for his claims (see chap. 1).

Jesus Believed in the Use of Miracles

Jesus repeatedly used miracles to confirm his claim to be the Son of God (see chap. 2). In Mark 2:10–11 he explicitly makes the connection between the two: "But that you may know that the Son of Man has power on earth to forgive sins . . . I say to you, arise, take up your bed, and go to your house" (NKJV). Likewise, when John the Baptist sends his disciples to ask Jesus if he is the promised Messiah, Jesus replies, "Go and tell John what you hear and see: The blind receive their sight and the lame walk, the lepers are cleansed and the deaf hear, and the dead are raised up" (Matt. 11:4–5 ESV). The Jewish leader Nicodemus acknowledges this point when he says, "Rabbi, we know that you are a teacher come from God; for no one can do these signs that You do unless God is with him" (John 3:2 NKJV). Jesus's miracles set him apart from all other religious leaders and were well attested to by first-generation eyewitnesses who recorded or transmitted a very accurate account of his work.

Jesus Believed in the Apologetic Use of the Resurrection

Given the monotheistic context in which Jesus spoke, the resurrection was another key element of his apologetic. Jesus skillfully taught that the Old Testament predicted the resurrection of the Messiah (Pss. 2:7; 16:10), and many times he predicted his own death and resurrection (Matt. 12:40; 17:9; John 2:19–21). His resurrection fulfilled the messianic prophecies, demonstrated his authority over sin and death (1 Cor. 15:55), and was resounding proof he was who he claimed to be. He alone demonstrated authority over creation, sin, and death (see chap. 2).

Jesus Would Have Used Theistic Arguments

Jesus never had the occasion to deal directly with an agnostic or an atheist. But as discussed in chapter 8, we can deduce what he would have done from the Old Testament, which he believed to be the imperishable and infallible Word of God (Matt. 5:17–18; John 10:35), as well as from the apostles whom he taught. The psalmist refers to teleological evidence for God from the design of the heavens: "The heavens declare the glory of God; and the firmament shows His handiwork" (Ps. 19:1 NKJV). The apostle Paul, whom Jesus called and taught (see Gal. 1:1, 12), uses both a cosmological form of argument from creation to the Creator that left men and women "without excuse" (Rom. 1:19–29) and a moral argument from the moral law that is "written on their hearts" to a moral lawgiver (Rom. 2:12–15).

Jesus Used the Apologetic of Love

Jesus says, "By this all will know you are My disciples, if you have love for one another" (John 13:35 NKJV). He knows that love is the greatest virtue (Matt. 22:37–38) and that people are attracted by love and repelled by the lack thereof. Hence, he reminds his followers that love is the evidence of what his sacrificial life is all about. He also knows that many will meet his claims with skepticism and even hostility (Luke 16:31; John 12:37). Nonetheless, he chooses the loving thing to do, namely, not forcing his will on individuals but allowing them to choose to follow or reject him (Matt. 23:37).

Jesus realized that love is a great attraction to truth; it gives the warmth that makes otherwise unpalatable truth more digestible. He knew that truth without love is cold and unappealing and love without truth is unthinking. Jesus's desire was that people know the truth that would set them free. This is why love played such a crucial role in getting people to accept the liberating truth he proclaimed.

Jesus Believed in the Necessity of the Holy Spirit in Apologetics

Further, Jesus knew that apologetics as such can never accomplish the task of convincing people to accept the spiritual truths that can convert them to Christ. No one is convicted of sin (John 16:7–8) or converted to Christ apart from the work of the Holy Spirit (John 3:3–7). Also, the Holy Spirit inspired the truth of Scripture (Matt. 22:43) and is the only one who can teach these truths (John 14:26; 16:13) and make one wise unto salvation (2 Tim. 3:15). In short, Jesus knew that apologetics at best can only provide evidence, while it is the Holy Spirit alone who can bring about a change of heart and will.

Jesus Was a Classical Apologist

From the summary of the evidence presented earlier (chaps. 1–8), it is clear that if Jesus had spelled out his apologetics systematically, he would have held to a classical apologetics system. His thought contained all the elements of classical apologetics, which is embraced by St. Augustine, Anselm, Thomas Aquinas, John Calvin, Jonathan Edwards, B. B. Warfield, John Gerstner, Kenneth Kantzer, R. C. Sproul, and many others.[5] Classical apologists: (1) believe in the use of reason to establish the existence of God; (2) hold that miracles, which follow from a theistic belief, are necessary to establish the truth claims of Christianity; (3) affirm that good witnesses and other evidence are necessary for the reliability of the New Testament documents; (4) set forth Jesus's miracles as confirmation of his claim to be God. All these elements of classical apologetics are present explicitly (see chaps. 1–7) or implicitly (see chap. 8) in the apologetic of Jesus.

In addition to the needed logic of the classical approach, however, Jesus teaches us that in real life we need to begin with where people are, not with where we would like them to be. We also need to understand that all the evidence in the world will not bring anyone to Christ apart from the work of the Holy Spirit. In the same way that a vast array of miracles did not persuade the Egyptians to come to faith in the God of Abraham, even with the evidence of the numerous miracles Jesus performed in his lifetime, many still refused to believe (John 12:37). For this reason, Jesus would not comply with demands from hard-hearted Pharisees (Matt. 12:38–40; see also Luke 16:19–31); but on the other hand, he does not rebuke Thomas for his doubts because his heart is still open (John 20:28; see also vv. 24–29). Jesus knew not only how to defend his claims but when to and when not to.

In conclusion, Jesus was not only the master teacher, he was also the master apologist. He did not expect people to believe without evidence. He never commended anyone for blind faith. Indeed, they were condemned for refusing to accept the evidence he offered. Of course, Jesus knew that evidence alone could not convert anyone. It could provide a basis for rational belief that he was the Son of God, but only the Holy Spirit, with the cooperation of the human will, could persuade a person to believe in him. Nonetheless, apologetic evidence provides the necessary condition for salvation, while only Spirit-induced saving faith produces the sufficient condition for it.

In practice, Jesus offered many different apologetic techniques, depending on what was needed on the occasion. Nonetheless, when an attempt to make an overall synthesis of Jesus's apologetics, Jesus fit better in the category of classical apologetics that incorporates both rational and historical evidence. And on any counting, Jesus's methods of attempting to convince people of his claims were not only multiple but masterful. Like his teaching techniques, Jesus's apologetic strategies are a model for all others who wish to fulfill the biblical imperative to be set in "defense of the gospel" (Phil. 1:16) and to "contend for the faith" once for all delivered to the saints (Jude 3).

Notes

Chapter 1 Jesus's Apologetic Use of Testimony

1. Leon Morris, *The New International Commentary on the New Testament: The Gospel according to John* (Grand Rapids: Eerdmans, 1971), 311.

2. Ibid., 313.

3. Ibid., 316.

4. W. F. Moulten, A. S. Geden, and H. K. Moulton, *Concordance to the Greek New Testament* (Edinburgh: T & T Clark, 1978), 617–18.

5. Gerhard Kittel and Gerhard Friedrich, *Theological Dictionary of the New Testament*, trans. and abridged Geoffrey Bromiley (Grand Rapids: Eerdmans, 1985), 566–68.

6. Morris, *New International Commentary*, 327.

7. D. A. Carson, *The Gospel according to John* (Grand Rapids: Eerdmans, 1991), 261.

8. Andrew Lincoln, *Truth on Trial* (Peabody, MA: Hendrickson, 2000), 78.

9. Ibid., 79.

10. Carson, *Gospel according to John*, 262.

11. Lincoln, *Truth on Trial*, 80.

12. Ibid., 81.

13. Carson, *Gospel according to John*, 266.

14. Russell, "Why I Am Not a Christian," in *The Basic Writings of Bertand Russell*, ed. Robert E. Egner (New York: Simon and Shuster, 1961), 593–94.

15. See Horace Bushnell, *The Character of Jesus: Forbidding His Possible Classification with Men* (New York: Chautauqua, 1888).

16. Bertrand Russell, "Why I Am Not a Christian," 586.

17. Bertrand Russell, "Why I Am an Agnostic," in *Basic Writings of Bertrand Russell*, ed. Egner, 579.

Chapter 2 Jesus's Apologetic Use of Miracles

1. Craig Blomberg, *Jesus and the Gospels: An Introduction and Survey* (Nashville: Broadman & Holman, 1997), 275.

2. Norman Geisler and Frank Turek, *I Don't Have Enough Faith to Be an Atheist* (Wheaton: Crossway, 2004), 201–2.

3. Dwight Pentecost, *The Words and Works of Christ* (Grand Rapids: Zondervan, 1981), 11.

4. Collin Brown, ed., *Dictionary of New Testament Theology*, vol. 2 (Grand Rapids: Zondervan, 1986), 626, 629.

5. John Witmer, *Immanuel* (Nashville: Word, 1998), 97–98.

6. Norman Geisler, *Baker Encyclopedia of Apologetics*, Baker Reference Library (Grand Rapids: Baker, 1999).

7. Tim LaHaye and Jerry Jenkins, *The Indwelling* (Wheaton: Tyndale, 2000), 364–68.

8. Leon Morris, *Tyndale New Testament Commentaries: Revelation* (Downers Grove, IL: InterVarsity, 1987), 162.

9. John Walvoord, *The Revelation of Jesus Christ* (Chicago: Moody, 1966), 208.

10. Ibid., 223–34.

11. Ibid., 224–26.

12. Ibid., 231–34.

13. Ron Nash, *Gospel and the Greeks* (Dallas: Word, 1992), 168.

14. J. Ed Komoszewski, M. James Sawyer, and Daniel B. Wallace, *Reinventing Jesus: How Contemporary Skeptics Miss the Real Jesus and Mislead Popular Culture* (Grand Rapids: Kregel, 2006), 235–36.

15. Gary Habermas, *The Historical Jesus* (Joplin, MO: College Press, 1997), 34.

16. Norman Geisler, *Survey of the New Testament* (Grand Rapids: Baker, 2008).

17. Carson, *Gospel according to John*, 393.

18. Ibid., 399.

19. D. A. Carson, *Matthew*, vol. 8 of *Expositor's Bible Commentary*, ed. Frank Gaebelein (Grand Rapids: Zondervan, 1984), 262.

20. A. N. Sherwin White, *Roman Society and Roman Law in the New Testament* (Oxford, England: Clarendon, 1963), 188–91.

21. William Lane Craig, *The Son Rises* (Chicago: Moody, 1981), 101.

22. Norman Geisler and Abdul Saleeb, *Answering Islam* (Grand Rapids: Baker, 1993), 164.

23. See Craig Blomberg, *The Historical Reliability of the Gospels* (Downers Grove, IL: InterVarsity, 1987); Gary Habermas, *The Historical Jesus: Ancient Evidence for the Life of Christ* (Joplin, MO: College Press, 1996).

24. David Hume, *An Enquiry Concerning Human Understanding* (New York: Liberal Arts Press, 1957), 118.

25. Geisler and Turek, *I Don't Have Enough Faith*.

26. Robert Jastrow, "A Scientist Caught between Two Faiths," an interview in *Christianity Today*, 6 August 1983, 15.

27. See Michael Behe, *Darwin's Black Box* (New York: Free Press, 1996); William Dembski, *The Design Revolution* (Downers Grove, IL: InterVarsity, 2004).

28. C. S. Lewis, *Mere Christianity* (New York: Macmillan, 1952).

29. See C. S. Lewis, *Miracles* (New York: Macmillan, 1947); Norman Geisler, *Miracles and Modern Thought* (Grand Rapids: Baker, 1992).

30. Geisler, *Baker Encyclopedia of Christian Apologetics*.

31. Hume, *Enquiry Concerning Human Understanding*, 129–30.

32. Geisler and Saleeb, *Answering Islam*, 164.

33. Geisler, *Baker Encyclopedia of Christian Apologetics*, 459.

Chapter 3 Jesus's Apologetic Use of the Resurrection

1. Josh McDowell, *The Resurrection Factor* (San Bernadino, CA: Here's Life Publishers, 1981), 66.

2. See Norman Geisler's critical review of Robert Price and Jeffrey Lowder, eds., *The Empty Tomb: Jesus beyond the Grave* (Amherst, NY: Prometheus, 2005) in *Christian Apologetics Journal* 5, no. 1 (spring 2006).

3. William McNeil, *A World History* (New York: Oxford University Press, 1979), 163.

4. David Strauss, *The Life of Jesus for the People*, 2nd ed. (London: Williams and Norgate, 1879), 1:412.

5. John Dominic Crossan, *Jesus, a Revolutionary Biography* (San Francisco: Harper Collins, 1989), 154.

6. Ibid., 156.

Chapter 4 Jesus's Apologetic Use of Reason

1. Aristotle, "Prior Analytics," in *The Basic Works of Aristotle* (New York: Random House, 1941).

2. See George Ladd, "The Greek versus the Hebrew View of Man," *Present Truth* (February 1977).

3. See Steven B. Cowan, "Aristotelian Logic in the Old Testament: A Biblical Refutation of a Strict Dichotomy between Greek and Hebrew Thought," *Bulletin of the Evangelical Philosophical Society* 14, no. 2 (1991): 21–30.

4. Dallas Willard, "Jesus the Logician," *Christian Scholars Review* (summer 1999): 610.

5. Norman Geisler, *Thomas Aquinas: An Evangelical Appraisal* (Eugene, OR: Wipf and Stock, 1991), 73.

6. See Norman Geisler and Ronald M. Brooks, *Come Let Us Reason: An Introduction to Logical Thinking* (Grand Rapids: Baker, 1990); Norman Geisler, *Systematic Theology*, vol. 1, *Introduction and Bible* (Grand Rapids: Baker, 2002), chap. 5.

7. Ibid., 73.

8. See Norman Geisler, "God, Evidence for," in *Baker Encyclopedia of Christian Apologetics*.

9. J. P. Moreland and William Lane Craig, *Philosophical Foundations for a Christian Worldview* (Downers Grove, IL: InterVarsity, 2003), 43.

10. James W. Sire, *Scripture Twisting* (Downers Grove, IL: InterVarsity, 1980), 17.

11. Roy B. Zuck, "The Role of the Holy Spirit in Hermeneutics," *Bibliotheca Sacra* 141 (April–June 1984): 126.

Chapter 5 Jesus's Apologetic Use of Parables

1. Philip Payne, "Interpreting Jesus' Parables" (Ph.D. dissertation, Cambridge University, 1980), 263.

2. Ibid., 313–17.

3. Simon Kistemaker, *The Parables* (Grand Rapids: Baker, 1980), 177.

4. Ibid., 86–90.

Chapter 6 Jesus's Apologetic Use of Discourse

1. See Blomberg, *Historical Reliability of the Gospels*, 166.

2. Stauffer, 184.

3. Cited in ibid., 179.

4. Ibid., 194–95.

5. Ibid., 186.

6. Carson, *Gospel according to John*, 289.

7. The essence of this section is parallel to Norman Geisler, "John, Historicity of," in *Baker Encyclopedia of Christian Apologetics*, 388–94.

Chapter 7 Jesus's Apologetic Use of Prophecy

1. See Barton Payne, *Encyclopedia of Biblical Prophecy* (Grand Rapids: Baker, 1987), 477–93.

2. Ibid., 501.

3. See Harold Hoehner, *Chronological Aspects of the Life of Christ* (Grand Rapids: Zondervan, 1978), 139.

Chapter 8 Jesus's Apologetic Use of Arguments for God

1. David Hume, *Letters of David Hume to William Strahan*, ed. G.Birkbeck Hill (Oxford, England: Clarendon Press, 1888), 1:187.

2. See Norman Geisler, *Knowing the Truth about Creation* (Eugene, OR: Wipf and Stock, 2003), appendix 1.

3. This is not to say that the Cause (God) is identical to his effects. That is impossible. God is infinite and his effects are finite. Hence, while God is like (i.e., similar to) his effects, there are also some significant differences. Anything in the effect that necessarily implies limitations or finitude does *not* bear any resemblance to God.

4. Immanuel Kant, *The Critique of Practical Reason*, trans. Lewis Beck (New York: Bobbs-Merrill, 1956), 166.

5. Russell, "Why I Am Not a Christian," 107.

6. Carl Sagan, *Pale Blue Dot* (New York: Ballantine, 1994), 7.

7. Cited in "Illustrations of the *Tao*," appendix to C. S. Lewis, *The Abolition of Man* (New York: Macmillan, 1947), 98.

Chapter 9 Jesus's Alleged Anti-Apologetic Passages

1. Kenneth Boa and Robert Bowman, *Faith Has Its Reasons* (Colorado Springs: NavPress, 2001), 364.

2. Leon Morris, *The Gospel according to Matthew* (Grand Rapids: Eerdmans, 1992), 324.

3. Carson, *Matthew*, 297.

4. William Hendriksen, *New Testament Commentary: Exposition of the Gospel according to Luke* (Grand Rapids: Baker, 1978), 782.

5. Darrell Bock, *Baker Exegetical Commentary on the New Testament: Luke* (Grand Rapids: Baker, 2002), 1376.

6. Carson, *Gospel according to John*, 659.

7. Blomberg, *Historical Reliability of the Gospels*, 56.

8. Gordon Fee, *The New International Commentary on the New Testament: The First Epistle to the Corinthians* (Grand Rapids: Eerdmans, 1987), 92.

9. Ibid., 343.

10. Ibid., 92.

11. Barclay Moon Newman, *Concise Greek-English Dictionary of the New Testament* (Stuttgart, Germany: Deutsche Bibelgesellschaft, United Bible Societies, 1993), 41.

12. Spiros Zodhiates, *The Complete Word Study Dictionary: New Testament*, Word Study Series, electronic ed. (Chattanooga: AMG Publishers, 2000, 1992, 1993), 1209.

13. Timothy Friberg, Barbara Friberg, and Neva F. Miller, *Analytical Lexicon of the Greek New Testament*, Baker's Greek New Testament Library, vol. 4 (Grand Rapids: Baker, 2000), 107.

14. Fee, *New International Commentary*, 116.

15. Friberg, Friberg, and Miller, *Analytical Lexicon*, 99.

16. Blomberg, *Historical Reliability of the Gospels*, 67.

17. Harold Hoehner, *Ephesians: An Exegetical Commentary* (Grand Rapids: Baker, 2002), 308.

18. Norman Geisler, *Chosen but Free* (Minneapolis: Bethany, 1999), 58.

19. F. F. Bruce, *The New International Commentary on the New Testament: The Epistle to the Hebrews* (Grand Rapids: Eerdmans, 1991), 276.

20. Ibid., 286–87.

Chapter 10 Jesus's Life as an Apologetic

1. Tacitus, *Annals*, 15:44.

2. Suetonius, *Life of Claudius*, 25; *Life of Nero*, 16.

3. Josephus, *Antiquities of the Jews*, 20:9.

4. Ibid., 18:3.

5. Origen, *Contra Celsum*, 1:47.

6. The authenticity for the basic reference is supported by these facts: (1) There is good textual evidence for the mention of Jesus and no textual evidence against it. (2) The text is written in the style of Josephus. (3) Although some may claim that this text was written by a Christian pretending to be Josephus, wording (other than "he was Christ") does not appear to have come from a believer. (4) The passage fits its context both grammatically and historically. (5) The reference to Jesus in Josephus, *Antiquities*, 20, seems to presuppose that he was mentioned earlier. (6) The later possible interpolation does not negate the genuineness of the rest of the text.

7. Cited by Habermas, *Historical Jesus*, 186.

8. Pliny the Younger, *Letters*, X:96, quoted in *Letters*, vol. 2, trans. William Melmoth (Cambridge: Harvard University Press, 1935).

9. *Letters*, X:97, quoted in *Letters*, trans. Melmoth.

10. *Sanhedrin*, 43a, in *The Babylonian Talmud*, vol. 3, trans. I. Epstein (London: Soncino, 1935), 281; cited by Habermas, *Historical Jesus*, 195.

11. Lucian, *The Death of Pelegrine*, 11–13; cited in H. W. Fowler and F. G. Fowler, *The Works of Lucian of Samosata*, 4 vols. (Oxford: Clarendon, 1949).

12. From the British Museum, Syriac Manuscript, Additional 14, 658; cited by Habermas, *Historical Jesus*, 200.

13. Cited in "Illustrations of the *Tao*," Lewis, *The Abolition of Man*, 98.

14. Ibid., 97–103.

15. Ayn Rand, *For the New Intellectual* (New York: New American Library, 1961), 180.

16. See Russell, "Why I Am Not a Christian," 593–94.

17. See Bushnell, *Character of Jesus*, 74.

18. *Ellicott's Commentary on the Whole Bible*, vol. 6 (Grand Rapids: Zondervan, 1954), 51.

19. See Bushnell, *Character of Jesus*.

20. Russell, "Why I Am Not a Christian," 586.

21. Russell, "Why I Am an Agnostic," 579.

22. See Richard Gerrier, *The Gandhi Nobody Knows* (Nashville: Thomas Nelson, 1983).

23. Busnell, *Character of Jesus*, 66, 77.

24. In 1950 Mitsuo Fuchida was given the tract "I Was a Prisoner of Japan," written by Jake DeShazer (published by Bible Literature International, known then as the Bible Meditation League). DeShazer was one of the famous Doolittle Raiders whose plane went down after a raid over Japan. During forty months as a POW in Japan, DeShazer was given a Bible to read and became a Christian. He returned to Japan in 1948 and preached the Good News of salvation in the nation that had once held him captive. DeShazer's story inspired Fuchida to purchase a Bible, in which he read the words that led to his salvation.

After his salvation, Fuchida also wrote a tract telling his story. He relates that on April 14, 1950, he read Luke's account of Christ's crucifixion. "Right at that moment, I seemed to meet Jesus for the first time. I understood the meaning of His death as a substitute for my wickedness, and so in prayer, I requested Him to forgive my sins and change me from a bitter, disillusioned ex-pilot into a well-balanced Christian with purpose in living. . . . On that day, I became a new person. My complete view on life was changed by the intervention of the Christ I had always hated and ignored before." Mitsuo Fuchida, *From Pearl Harbor to Golgatha* (San Jose: Sky Pilots Press, 1953).

25. Busnell, *Character of Jesus*, 19.

Chapter 11 Jesus and the Role of the Holy Spirit in Apologetics

1. See Simon Greenleaf, *The Testimony of the Evangelist* (1784; repr., Grand Rapids: Baker, 1984); Frank Morrison, *Who Moved the Stone* (London: Faber & Faber, 1958); C. S. Lewis, *Mere Christianity* (New York: Macmillan, 1953). We also have records in our files of many agnostics and atheists who have come to Christ after reading one or more of our apologetics books. See, for example, Patrick Zukeran, *Unless I See: Reasons to Consider the Christian Faith* (Dallas: Brown Books, 2000); *World Religions* (Dallas: Probe Books, 2004); and Geisler, *Baker Encyclopedia of Christian Apologetics*; Geisler and Saleeb, *Answering Islam: The Crescent in Light of the Cross*, 2nd ed. (Grand Rapids: Baker, 2002); Geisler and Brooks, *Come, Let Us Reason*; Geisler and Joseph Holden, *Living Loud: Defending Your Faith* (Nashville: Broadman & Holman, 2002); Geisler and Peter Bocchino, *Unshakable Foundations* (Minneapolis: Bethany, 2001); Geisler and Brooks, *When Skeptics Ask* (Wheaton: Victor, 1990).

2. St. Augustine, *On Predestination*, 11.5.

3. Augustine, *Letters*, 120.1.

4. Augustine, *On the Gospel of John*, 27.9.

5. Augustine, *On the Creed*, 4.

6. Augustine, *On True Religion*, 36.

7. Augustine, *On the Trinity*, 8.4.9.

8. Augustine, *The City of God*, 22.8.

9. Aquinas, *Summa Theologica*, 1a, 3, 2.

10. Ibid., 2a2ae, 2, 10.

11. Aquinas, *Summa Contra Gentiles*, 1, 6.

12. Aquinas, *Commentary on Ephesians*, 96.

13. Aquinas, *On Truth*, 14, A1, ad 6.

14. Aquinas, *Summa Theologica*, 2a2ae, 6, 1.

15. Ibid., 2a2ae, 2, 9, ad 3.

16. Aquinas, *On Truth*, 14, 10, ad 11.

17. Aquinas, *Summa Theologica*, 2a2ae, 2, 2, ad 3.

18. Ibid., 2a2ae, 1, 4, ad 2.

19. Ibid., 2a2ae, 2, 1, reply.

20. Aquinas, *On Truth*, 14, 9, ad 4.

21. See Arvin Vos, *Aquinas, Calvin, and Contemporary Protestant Thought: A Critique of Protestant Views on the Thought of Thomas Aquinas*, foreword Ralph McInerny (Grand Rapids: Eerdmans, 1985).

22. John Calvin, *Institutes of the Christian Religion*, 1.5.1–2.

23. John Calvin, *Calvin's New Testament Commentaries: Epistle of Paul to the Romans and Thessalonicans*.

24. Calvin, *Institutes*, 1.8.1; emphasis added.

25. By *proof* Calvin does not mean an inescapable rational argument. Rather, he means sufficient evidence.

26. Calvin, *Institutes*, 1.8.1.

27. Ibid., 1.11.2.

28. Ibid., 1.7.1; cf. 1.8.1 and 1.7.4.

29. Ibid., 1.7.4.

30. Ibid., 1.7.5.

31. Ibid.

32. Ibid., 1.8.1.

33. R. C. Sproul, "The Internal Testimony of the Holy Spirit," in *Inerrancy*, ed. Norman Geisler (Grand Rapids: Zondervan, 1979), 341.

34. B. B. Warfield, *Selected Shorter Writings of Benjamin B. Warfield 1851–1921*, vol. 2, ed. John E. Meeter (Nutley, NJ: Presbyterian and Reformed, 1970–1973), 98.

35. Warfield, *Selected Shorter Writings*, vol. 9, 15.

36. Ibid.

37. See B. B. Warfield, *Biblical and Theological Studies*, ed. Samuel G. Craig (Philadelphia: Presbyterian and Reformed, 1952), chap. 16.

38. John Gerstner, "On Being," in *Jonathan Edwards: Representative Selections, with Introduction, Bibliography, and Notes*, ed. Clarence H. Faust and Thomas H. Johnson (New York: Hill and Wang, 1962), 22–23.

39. Jonathan Edwards, *Freedom of the Will*, part 2, section 3.

40. Ibid., no. 91, 74.

41. Jonathan Edwards, *The Works of Jonathan Edwards*, ed. Edward Hickman, vol. 1, 97.

42. John Gerstner, *Jonathan Edwards: A Mini-Theology* (Soli Deo Gloria Ministries, 1997), 27.

43. Jonathan Edwards, "Miscellanies," in *The Works of Jonathan Edwards, with a Memoir by Sereno E. Dwight*, rev. Edward Hickman (Carlisle, PA: Banner of Truth Trust, 1974), 1.1.19.

44. Ibid., 1.6.15.

45. Ibid., 1.6.16.

46. Ibid., 1.6.22.

47. See Edwards, "Of Being," *The Works of Jonathan Edwards*, vol. 1, 295–97.

Chapter 12 Jesus's Apologetic Method

1. Sometimes this is expressed by the Greek word *en* (in) and sometimes by *eis* (into), as in John 3:16. Other times we are asked simply to believe him. But the point is the same: It is not sufficient to simply believe *that* Christ is the Son of God; we must also place our trust *in* him to take us to heaven. As James points out, the demons believe that (*hoti*) God exists, and yet they are lost (James 2:19).

2. See the article on "Van Till, Cornelius," in Geisler, *Baker Encyclopedia of Christian Apologetics*.

3. Ibid.

4. See article on "Clark, Gordon," in Geisler, *Baker Encyclopedia of Christian Apologetics*.

5. See articles on "Apologetics," in Geisler, *Baker's Encyclopedia of Christian Apologetics*.

Norman L. Geisler (PhD, Loyola University of Chicago) is cofounder and former dean of Southern Evangelical Seminary. He is the author of more than seventy books, including the *Baker Encyclopedia of Christian Apologetics*.

Patrick Zukeran (ThM, Dallas Theological Seminary) is a research associate and a national and international speaker for Probe Ministries.